Hello and welcome!

Nachdem du neue Wörter in der Schule besprochen hast, kannst du die **New words** in diesem Buch als Vokabelheft benutzen.

Hello and welcome! Ich bin der Wordmaster und helfe dir beim Wörterlernen.

Die **fett gedruckten** deutschen Wörter sind Lernwörter. Sie fehlen im englischen Satz, damit du sie eintragen kannst.

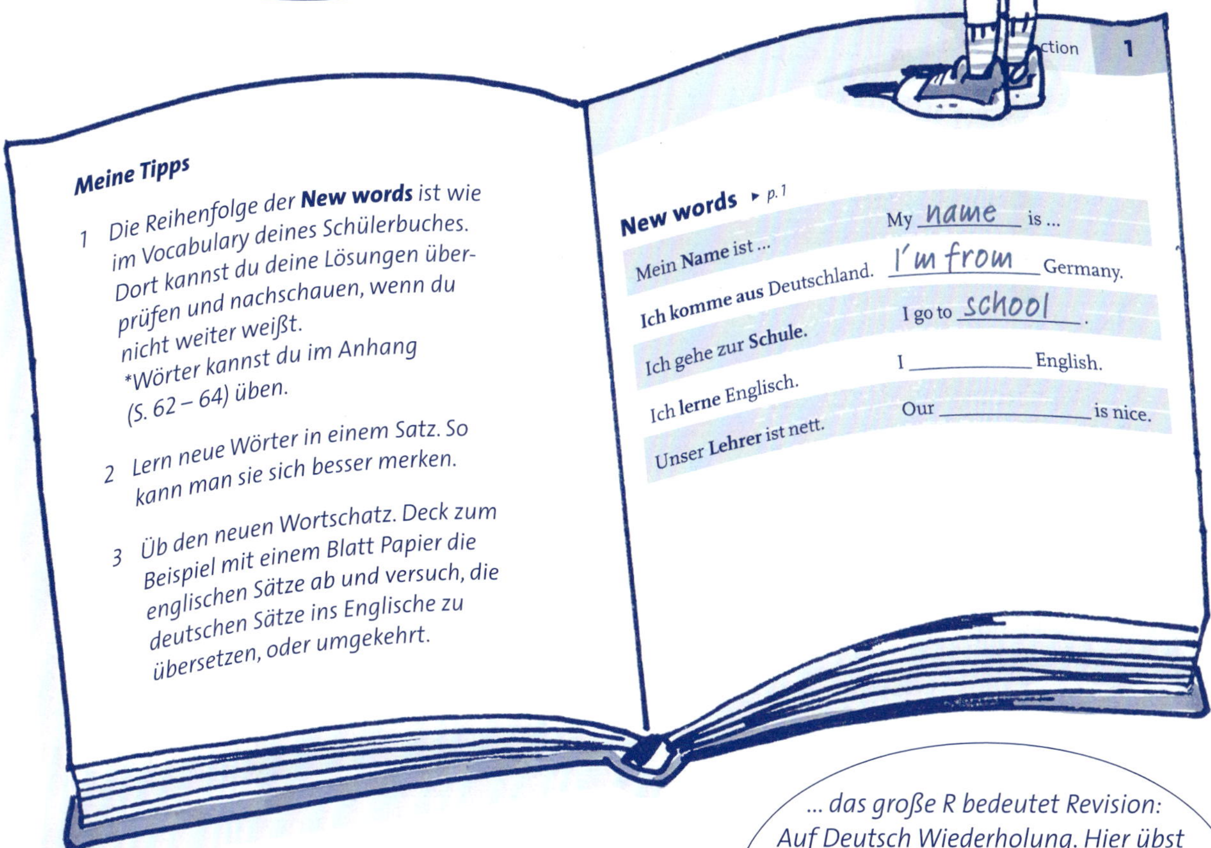

... das große R bedeutet Revision: Auf Deutsch Wiederholung. Hier übst du Vokabeln, die du bereits früher gelernt hast.

Hi! Ich bin Ken und gebe dir Tipps. Zum Beispiel ...

Überhaupt: Es gibt neben **New words** viele lustige Übungen. Die Lösungen findest du im beigelegten Heftchen.

Introduction

New words ▸ pp. 6 – 7

Hast du schon die **Einführung** gelesen?	Have you read the ______________ yet?
Wir haben viel Spaß in unserer **Jugend**gruppe.	We have lots of fun in our ____________ group.
Dieser Fußballstar ist ein **National**held.	This football star is a ______________ hero.
Wer ist dein Lieblings**musiker**?	Who is your favourite ______________ ?
Wird er **am** Konzert **teilnehmen**?	Will he ______________ the concert?
Ist Wales ein Teil des Vereinten **Königreiches**?	Is Wales part of the ______________ ?
Wir trafen Menschen **aus der ganzen** Welt.	We met people ______________ .
Magst du diese **Art von** Musik?	Do you like this ______________ music?
Magst du auch **klassische** Musik?	Do you like ____________ music too?
Kannst du **Schlagzeug** spielen?	Can you play ______________ ?
Ist es schwierig, **Geige** zu spielen?	Is it difficult to play ______________ ?
Mein Vater spielt **Fiedel** in einer Band.	My dad plays ______________ in a band.
Im Moment **fährt** er **voll auf** walisische Musik **ab**.	He'__________ Welsh music at the moment.
Übrigens habe ich mir eine Gitarre gekauft.	______________ , I've bought a guitar.

1 Crossword

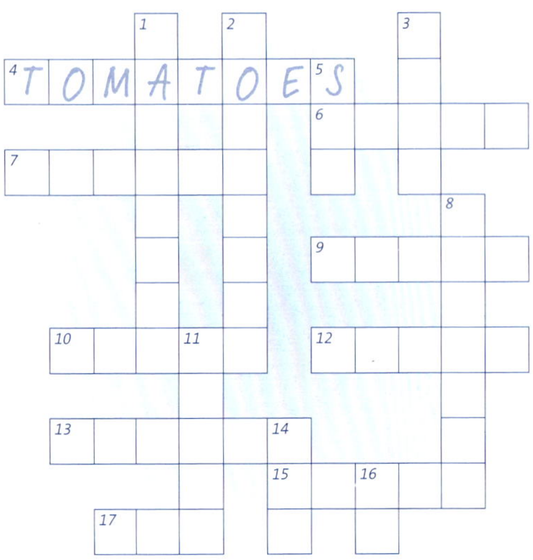

Across

4 They're round, red and go in ★ salads. (8)
6 very bad, terrible (5)
7 go – went / catch – ★ (6)
9 somebody who steals things (5)
10 You can keep money in this. (5)
12 opposite of 'clean' (5)
13 go – went / become – ★
15 opposite of 'quiet' (5)
17 You can wear this on your head. (3)

Down

1 build – building / laugh – ★ (7)
2 German – weitermachen / English – ★ (8)
3 A woman who is married to a man is his ★. (4)
5 opposite of 'happy' (3)
8 100 years (7)
11 another word for 'begin' (5)
14 opposite of 'beginning' (3)
16 short form of 'Information technology' (2)

New words ▸ *pp. 8 – 9*

Wir verbrachten die Woche in einer **Herberge**.	We spent the week in a ______________ .
Kannst du ein **Instrument** spielen?	Can you play an ______________ ?
Aus welchem Land kommt das **Steeldrum**?	What country is the ______________ from?
Man braucht **Stahl** um Brücken zu bauen.	You need ______________ to build bridges.
Dieses Lied hat eine schöne **Melodie**.	This song has got a nice ______________ .
Unsere Band **hat** jeden Monat **einen Auftritt**.	Our band ______________ every month.
Ich habe die Karten an der Theater**kasse** gekauft.	I bought the tickets at the ______________ .
eine **Mischung** aus Jazz und klassischer Musik	a ______________ of jazz and classical music
Wir spielen nicht nur **westliche** Musik.	We don't just play ______________ music.

2 Verb forms

Ergänze die Tabelle der unregelmäßigen Verben.

1	keep	kept	kept
2		showed	
3	spend		
4	hide		
5		did	
6			taken

7	fly		
8		read	
9			thrown
10			spoken
11		wrote	
12	ride		

3 Lost words

Ergänze die Sätze mit den Wörtern im Feuerwerk.

1 ____________ his youth grandpa was a very good swimmer.

2 What kind ____________ music do your parents like?

3 People ____________ all over Germany came to the concert.

4 What's the shortest way ____________ the hostel?

5 There were three different bands ______________ the gig.

6 ______________ the way, where did you buy the steel drum?

7 London is famous ______________ its pop concerts.

New words ▸ *pp. 10 – 11*

Warst du jemals in den **Vereinigten Staaten**?	Have you been to the ______________________ ?
Mein Freund **legt** jedes Wochenende **Platten auf**.	My friend _____ every weekend.
Hast du im **Workshop** viel gelernt?	Did you learn much at the ___________ ?
Nett, dich kennenzulernen.	____________________________________
Eine halbe Stunde später kam er.	He came ___________________ later.
Er gab mir die **Hälfte** seiner Brote.	He gave me ___________ of his sandwiches.
Kannst du mir die Bilder **mailen**?	Can you ___________ me the pictures?
Lass uns **in Verbindung bleiben**.	Let's ___________________________________ .
Wird Tim auf der Party sein?– **Wart's ab!**	Will Tim be at the party? – ___________________
eine neue **Aufnahme** eines alten Lieds	a new _________________________ of an old song
Welches Bild **passt zu** welchem Wort?	Which picture ________________ which word?
Er spielt **Cello** in einer **Band**.	He plays ___________________ in a ___________ .
Ich mag den Klang einer **Klarinette**.	I like the sound of a ___________ .
eine **Bass-** und eine **elektrische** Gitarre	a ___________ and an __________________ guitar
Spielst du **Querflöte** oder **Blockflöte**?	Do you play the ___________ or the ___________ ?
Wann hat er angefangen **Saxophon** zu spielen?	When did he start to play ___________________ ?
Ist dies eine **Posaune** oder eine **Trompete**?	Is this a _____________ or a _____________ ?

4 Last letter – first letter

Der letzte Buchstabe von jedem Wort ist gleichzeitig der erste des nächsten Wortes.

1 Trommel
2 Mischung
3 elektrisch
4 Konzert
5 Trompete
6 Posaune
7 genug
8 Hälfte
9 Fiedel
10 Aufzug (AE)
11 Blockflöte

5 Word search

Finde und markiere die 10 Musikinstrumente im Gitter. Gib dann ihre deutschen Übersetzungen an. (↓ →)

W	Y	H	D	T	K	X	Z	L	N
M	Y	Q	R	T	K	K	W	M	R
J	O	O	U	F	I	D	D	L	E
T	R	O	M	B	O	N	E	F	C
P	T	R	U	M	P	E	T	L	O
I	C	G	N	H	F	B	D	U	R
A	Z	C	E	L	L	O	M	T	D
N	V	N	U	U	H	P	Z	E	E
O	G	U	I	T	A	R	B	K	R
S	A	X	O	P	H	O	N	E	Y

drum – Trommel ____________________

____________________ ____________________

____________________ ____________________

____________________ ____________________

____________________ ____________________

6 Word groups

Trage die Wörter von der Wiese in die richtigen Kletterseile ein.

Unit 1

New words ▸ p. 12

London ist die **Hauptstadt** von Großbritannien.	London is the ____ of Great Britain.
Wer kann uns in der Stadt **herumführen**?	Who can ____ us ____ the city?
Die Aussicht vom **Riesenrad** aus ist toll.	The view from the ____ is fantastic.
Schau, dieses Auto hat nur drei **Räder**.	Look. This car has only got three ____ .
In einer Jugendherberge kann **man** billig wohnen.	____ can stay cheaply at a youth hostel.
Man sagt, das Essen hier ist sehr gut.	____ the food is very good here.
eine **Tondatei** kopieren	copy a ____
Obwohl wir gut spielten, verloren wir.	____ we played well, we lost.
Wohnt die **Königin** in diesem Schloss?	Does the ____ live in this palace?
Hast du letzte Nacht von mir **geträumt**?	Did you ____ about me last night?

1 Definitions

Vervollständige die Definitionen mit Wörtern aus den Mauersteinen. Trage die richtigen Wörter aus Kens Zeitung in die rechte Spalte ein.

	important	hotel	country	four	photos	computer	use	
piano	spend	stage	king	~~move~~	places	live	woman	listen

1 A car needs them to *move* and usually has ____ of them. *wheels*

2 the most ____ city in a ____ ____

3 interesting ____ in a city: tourists often take ____ of them ____

4 an important ____ , often the wife of a ____ ____

5 a place to ____ the night, usually cheaper than a ____ ____

6 ____ music, usually on a ____ , for people to enjoy ____

7 a thing like a ____ or flute, which you ____ to make music ____

8 a ____ file with a recording you can ____ to ____

New words ▸ p. 13

trockenes Wetter, aber **ziemlich** kühl für den Juni	dry weather, but ________ cool for June
Wieviele **Bezirke** hat London?	How many ____________ has London got?
Auf einem **Flohmarkt** kann man alte Dinge kaufen.	You can buy old things at a ______________ .
Kleider **aus zweiter Hand** sind oft billig.	________________ clothes are often cheap.
Ich **horchte aufs** Telefon, aber es klingelte nicht.	I ____________ the phone, but it didn't ring.
Versuche das **Wesentliche** zu verstehen.	Try and understand the ________ .
Im Allgemeinen musst du dir nicht	______________ you don't have to
... jede **Einzelheit** eines Textes merken.	... remember every __________ of a text.
eine **genaue** Beschreibung geben	give an ______________ description
Er sah das Feuer im Zimmer und **geriet in Panik**.	He saw the fire in the room and __________ .
ein guter **Tipp** für Touristen	a good ________ for tourists

2 Crossword: places in a city

Die Buchstabenrätsel helfen dir, die Lösungen zu finden. (↓ →)

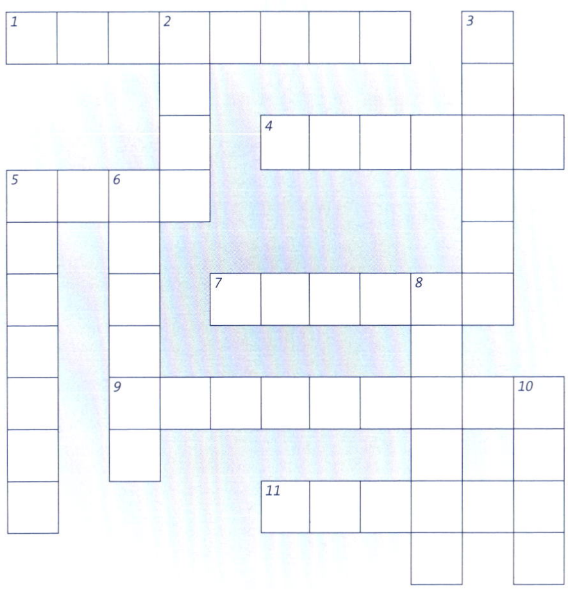

Across

1 ISOPHTAL: You can get help here if you're ill. (8)
4 EUUMMS: Go to this place to see old and interesting things. (6)
5 KCLO: a kind of lift for boats (4)
7 CAPELA: Kings and queens live here. (6)
9 DALERCATH: a very important church (9)
11 MOLCUN: There's a statue of Nelson on top of one. (6)

Down

2 KRAP: Go here to walk, relax or play. (4)
3 SERQUA: a place with buildings on four sides (6)
5 RIBALRY: You can find lots of books here. (7)
6 RUCHCH: a building, often with a tower – some people go there on Sundays (6)
8 SICCUR: a round place with buildings around it (6)
10 NALE: a kind of road (4)

New words ▸ pp. 14–15

eine **Fahrkarte** für den Zug kaufen	buy a ____________ for the train
Wir brauchen eine Fahrkarte für zwei **Zonen**.	We need a ticket for two __________ .
Mit einer **Tagesfahrkarte** sind die Busse billiger.	With a __________________ the buses are cheaper.
die Hauptstädte von **Mittel**europa besuchen	visit the capitals of _______________ Europe
In London fahre ich immer mit der **U-Bahn**.	In London I always travel by __________ .
Wie komme ich am besten dahin?	____ ?
Fahren alle **Linien** in die Stadtmitte?	Do all _____________ go to the city centre?
Nimm die Victoria Line **in Richtung Norden**.	Take the Victoria Line ____________________ .
Ihr müsst am Piccadilly Circus **umsteigen**.	You have to _____________ at Piccadilly Circus.
Hohe Gebäude haben meistens einen Fahrstuhl.	_______________ buildings usually have a lift.
Fakten und Daten sind in Geschichte sehr wichtig.	________ and dates are very important in history.

3 Word ladder

Gehe von unten nach oben, indem du bei jeder Sprosse einen Buchstaben veränderst.

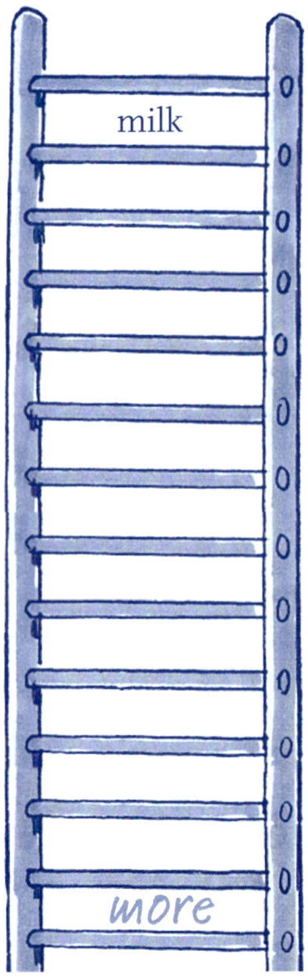

Do you take ★ in your tea?

1.6 km = 1 ★.

This pen isn't ★? Is it yours?

good, OK

Which underground ★ can I take to the cathedral?

We live in the little house at the end of this ★.

the opposite of 'early'

How clean is the water in this ★?

What's the food ★ at this restaurant? – Really good!

It's more fun to listen to ★ music than to a CD.

the opposite of 'hate'

leave the place where you have lived and go to live in another place

the opposite of 'less'

4 More about ... London Underground

Vervollständige den Text mit den Wörtern aus der Box.

~~also~~	although	and	because	
before	but	more	only	too	when

London Underground is the oldest underground railway in the world. People also (1) call it the 'Tube' __________ (2) the tunnels look like *tubes. The first line opened in 1863. It was __________ (3) six kilometres long. The first electric trains came in 1890; __________ (4) that, there were *steam trains. Today there are 12 lines __________ (5) 275 stations. Together all the lines are 408 kilometres long, __________ (6) only 185 kilometres are actually under the ground. Outside the city centre, the lines run over ground __________ (7). In 1863, __________ (8) the Underground opened, 41,000 people travelled on the first day. Today __________ (9) than 3 million people use the Tube every day. __________ (10) it's more expensive than the bus and you don't see as much of London, it's the fastest way to travel around the city.

tube = Röhre; steam train= Dampfzug; actually = tatsächlich

5 Word friends

In jedem Haus gibt es drei Wörter bzw. Wortverbindungen, die man direkt nach dem Verb auf der Fahne benutzen kann. Unterstreiche sie.

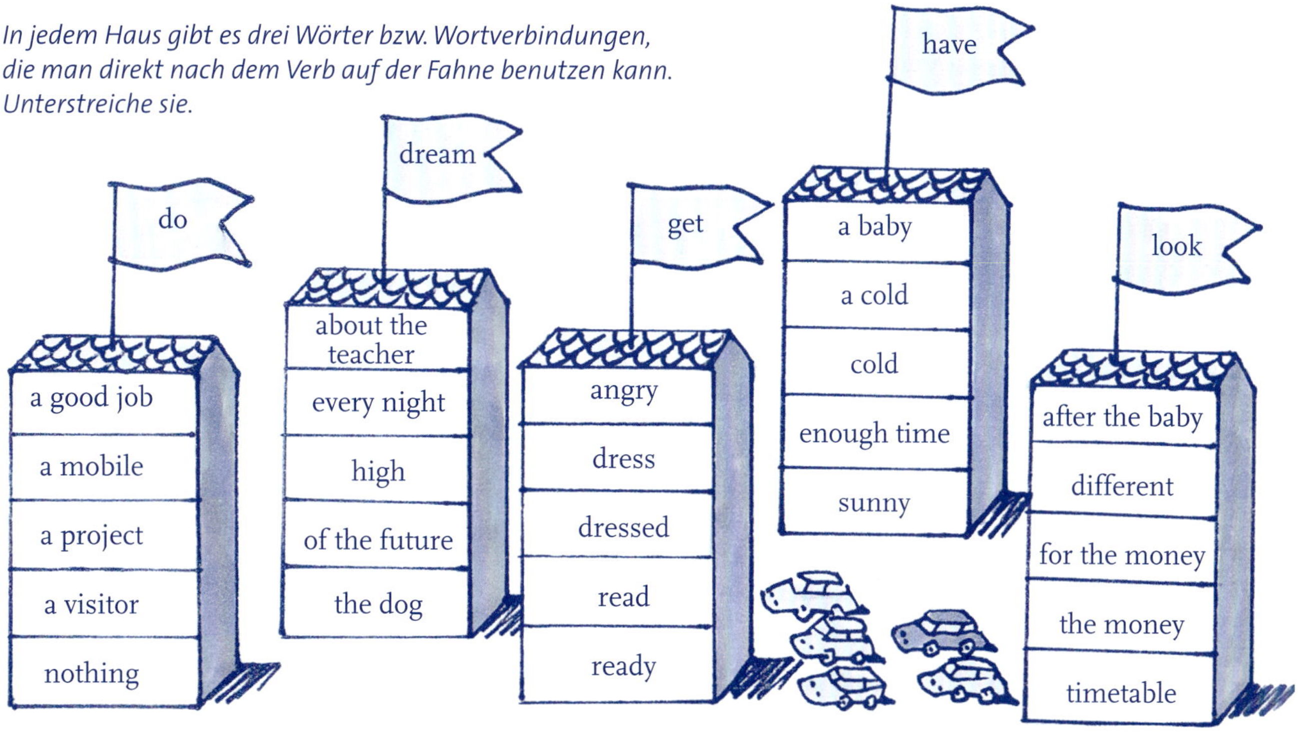

New words ▸ p. 16

Mein Fahrrad ist kaputt. Ich werde **zu Fuß gehen.**	My bike is broken. I'll ______ .
Jack! Deine **Mutti** ruft aus New York an!	Jack! Your ______ is calling from New York!
Ruf mich auf meinem **Handy** an.	Call me on my ______ .
eine **Überraschung** als Geburtstagsgeschenk	a ______ as a birthday present
Das große Gebäude da drüben ist eine **Moschee.**	The big building over there is a ______ .
Wo kann ich die **Synagoge** finden?	Where can I find the ______ ?
Ich mag keine heißen **Mahlzeiten** am Abend.	I don't like hot ______ in the evening.
Kann ich bitte die **Speisekarte** haben?	Can I have the ______ , please?
ein Wort im Wörterbuch **nachschlagen**	______ a word in the dictionary
Für dieses Wort gibt es keinen **Eintrag.**	There's no ______ for this word.
ein **mildes** oder **mittelscharfes Gericht**	a ______ or ______
Ich esse keine Äpfel – ich bin **allergisch gegen** sie.	I don't eat apples – I'm ______ them.
Ich liebe Schokolade mit **Nüssen.**	I love chocolate with ______ .
Sind **Linsen** ein Art **Gemüse**?	Are ______ a kind of ______ ?
Es hat geregnet, aber jetzt ist es wieder **trocken.**	It rained, but it's ______ again now.
Es gibt eine leckere Kräuter**soße** zum Fisch.	There's a delicious herb ______ with the fish.

6 One or two letters?

Trage die fehlenden Buchstaben ein: **d** *oder* **dd**, **f** *oder* **ff**

d/dd	fi__le	mi__le	stu__ent	hi__en	rea__y	mo__el
f/ff	a__raid	gira__e	tra__ic	o__ten	di__icult	le__t
n/nn	a__orak	begi__ing	di__er	tu__el	le__til	pe__cil

7 The fourth word

Welches Wort fehlt hier?

1 cello – instrument / palace – building

2 banana – fruit / carrot – ______

3 hot – cold / dry – ______

4 mum – mom / mobile phone – ______

5 sleep – tired / drink – ______

6 wife – husband / king – ______

8 Word building

Verbinde ein Wort aus der Liste mit einem Wort auf den Noten. Trage die deutsche Übersetzung ein.

1 dancing lessons Tanzstunden
2 family ______ ______
3 sports ______ ______
4 sound ______ ______
5 ice ______ ______
6 film ______ ______
7 doorbell ______
8 class ______ ______
9 home ______ ______
10 wheel ______ ______
11 fire ______ ______
12 week ______ ______

9 Odd word out

Ein Wort passt nicht. Finde und unterstreiche es.

1 mosque – synagogue – museum – church
2 car – wheel – bike – bus
3 recorder – CD player – trombone – flute
4 national – sweet – mild – spicy
5 breakfast – lunch – menu – dinner
6 nut – carrot – meal – lentil

10 The best word

Finde das Wort in der Strickleiter, das am besten in die Lücke passt.

1 Why are you so ______ with me? I haven't done anything wrong.
2 Paul is so ______ . He even finds it hard to say hello to people.
3 Kim felt very ______ when she won the first prize.
4 Rob looked ______ . He didn't understand the joke.
5 Don't be ______ . The dog really isn't dangerous.
6 We were a bit ______ before the test, but it was actually OK.

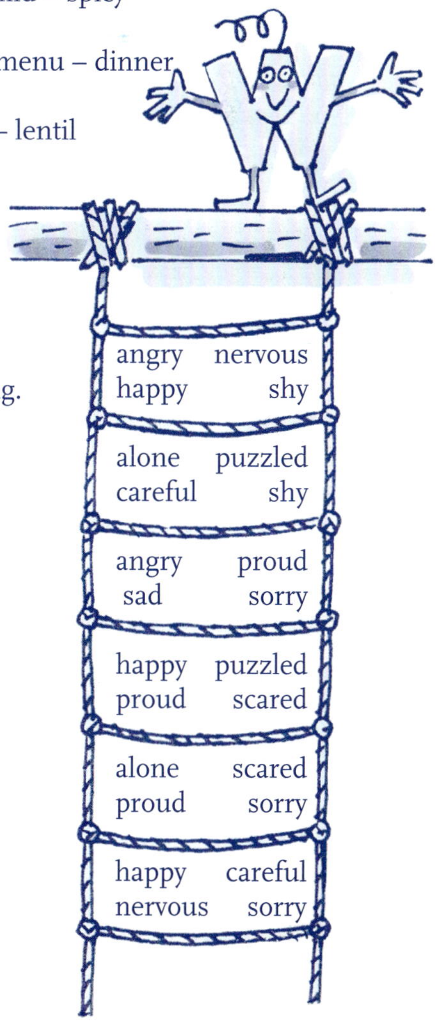

New words ▸ p. 17

ein Foto von einem **Straßenkünstler** machen	take a photo of a ______________
Sie ist **seit** Dienstag im Urlaub.	She's been on holiday ______________ Tuesday.
Er bewegt sich nicht – er **scheint** verletzt zu sein.	He isn't moving – he ______________ to be hurt.
Er gähnt. Er sieht aus, **als ob** er müde ist.	He's yawning. He looks ______________ he's tired.
Wir warten hier **seit** acht Stunden.	We've been waiting here ______________ 8 hours.
Wir wohnen in einer ruhigen **Gegend**.	We live in a quiet ______________ .
Mamas Kuchen sind immer so **lecker**.	Mum's cakes are always so ______________ .
Ohne Stadtplan **verlaufe** ich **mich** immer.	I always ______________ without a map.
Danke! Das ist eine wirklich **tolle** Idee.	Thanks! That's a really ______________ idea.
Es war billig – nur **ein paar** Pfund!	It was cheap – only ______________ pounds!
Eine große **Menge** Fans warteten auf den Popstar.	A big ______________ of fans waited for the pop star.
Viele der Straßenkünstler waren **Akrobaten**.	Lots of the street performers were ______________ .
Er **lief** in der Stadt **herum** und machte Fotos.	He ______________ the city and took photos.

11 Word search

Finde im Rätsel 16 deutsche Begriffe zum Thema Verkehr.
Schreibe dann das deutsche Wort und die englische Übersetzung auf.
(↓ →)

S	T	R	A	S	S	E	N	B	A	H	N
U	D	B	A	H	N	H	O	F	M	U	M
E	I	N	S	T	E	I	G	E	N	M	Q
F	L	U	G	H	A	F	E	N	C	S	A
L	F	A	H	R	R	A	D	H	I	T	U
U	Q	F	L	U	G	Z	E	U	G	E	T
G	Q	T	A	X	I	J	Q	H	F	I	O
S	F	A	H	R	P	L	A	N	A	G	P
T	Z	A	U	S	S	T	E	I	G	E	N
E	Z	T	B	U	S	W	U	E	U	N	E
I	U	F	M	S	F	A	E	H	R	E	K
G	G	B	A	H	N	S	T	E	I	G	T

Straßenbahn – tram

______________ ______________ ______________

New words ▸ *pp. 20–25*

ein **Verkehrsmittel**projekt für das Stadtzentrum	a ______________ project for the city centre
Nach 57 Tagen auf dem Meer sahen sie **Land**.	After 57 days at sea they saw ____________ .
Maulwürfe leben in Tunneln unter dem **Erdboden**.	Moles live in tunnels under the ____________ .
War diese **Durchsage** für unseren Zug?	Was that ________________ for our train?
Ich will einen Englisch**kurs** in England machen.	I want to do an English __________ in England.
Jo war nach seinem Urlaub **sonnengebräunt**.	Jo ____________________ after his holiday.
Der Strand ist im Sommer oft **überfüllt**.	The beach is often ______________ in summer.
Ich **wünschte**, wir hätten längere Sommerferien.	I ____________ we had longer summer holidays.
Wir sind bloß eine normale **Alltags**familie.	We're just a normal ______________ family.

12 Hidden words

*Ergänze die Wortgruppen, indem du Wörter mit Buchstaben des Wortes **„parliament"** bildest.*

13 Word families

Finde die passenden Verben zu den angegebenen Nomen.

1 dream – dream

2 explanation – ____________

3 installation – ____________

4 winner – ____________

5 laughter – ____________

6 building – ____________

7 description – ____________

8 rehearsal – ____________

New words ▸ p. 26

Wie **funktioniert** diese Maschine?	How does this machine ____________ ?
Es ist sicherer, einen **Helm** zu tragen.	It's safer to wear a ____________ .
Taten sprechen mehr als Worte.	____________ speak louder than words.
Auf dem **Schild** steht, dass der Laden offen ist.	The ____________ says that the shop is open.
Das muss ich mir **genau** anschauen.	I'll have to look ____________ at that.
Drück auf den **Knopf** und die Tür wird aufgehen.	Push the ____________ and the door will open.
Er ging weg, **erschien** aber bald wieder.	He went away, but soon ____________ again.
Es ist **irgendwie unheimlich** nachts im Park.	It's ____________ in the park at night.
einen Bericht über einen **Mord** lesen	read a report on a ____________
Keiner weiß, wer die Frau **ermordet** hat.	Nobody knows who ____________ the woman.
Werden sie den **Mörder** fangen?	Will they catch the ____________ ?
Können wir den Unfall**opfern** helfen?	Can we help the ____________ of the accident?

14 Pronunciation

Ordne die Wörter aus der Box der richtigen Aussprachegruppe zu.

~~already~~ beach appear bread breakfast cheap ~~clean~~ clear dead ~~dear~~ hear ear eastbound head idea leave meant tea

e	iː	ɪə
already	clean	dear

New words ▸ pp. 27–29

Ist das **Blut** oder Ketchup auf deinem Hemd?	Is that __________ or ketchup on your shirt?
Ist das eine Maus oder eine **Ratte**?	Is that a mouse or a __________ ?
Dieser Plan ist nicht sehr **realistisch**.	This plan isn't very __________ .
Sei nicht so aufgeregt. Entspann dich **einfach**!	Don't be so nervous. __________ relax!
Zieh bitte den **Stecker** nicht heraus.	Please don't pull out the __________ .
Ohne **Strom** funktioniert kein Computer.	No computer works without __________ .
ein **Lichtblitz** am Himmel	a __________ in the sky
nahe am Meer, und nicht weit von London	__________ the sea, and not far from London
Der Baum warf einen **Schatten** auf das Feld.	The tree threw a __________ on the field.
Er hatte ein gefährliches **Messer** in der Hand.	He had a dangerous __________ in his hand.
Es ist dunkel! Schalt das **Licht** bitte ein.	It's dark. Please turn on the __________ .
Wer **kümmert sich um** die Kinder?	Who's __________ the children?
Geh weg vom Herd – er ist noch sehr heiß.	__________ from the cooker. It's still very hot.
Die Geschichte hatte ein unglückliches **Ende**.	The story had an unhappy __________ .
meiner Ansicht nach ...	__________ ...
Jo ist **nicht mehr** hier – er ist gestern gegangen.	Jo is ___ here __________ . He left yesterday.
Wie komme ich voran?	__________

15 Opposites

Trage die Gegenteile der fett gedruckten Wörter in die Lücken ein.

1 an **international** / a national festival

2 Do you like **mild** / __________ dishes?

3 This room is very **dirty** / __________ .

4 Turn **left** / __________ at the next corner.

5 a story with a good **beginning** / __________

6 The victim was an **old** / a __________ man.

7 He's the **best** / __________ singer I've ever heard.

8 give the **correct** / __________ answer

9 It's **possible** / __________ to get there by bus.

10 Are you planning to **arrive** / __________ early?

11 Only **poor** / __________ people live in this street.

12 Is the supermarket **open** / __________ ?

13 a **noisy** / __________ street

14 a **wet** / __________ towel

15 This is my **wife** / __________ .

16 **strong** / __________ tea

15 Hour glasses

Übersetze die Wörter und trage sie in die passende Sanduhr ein.

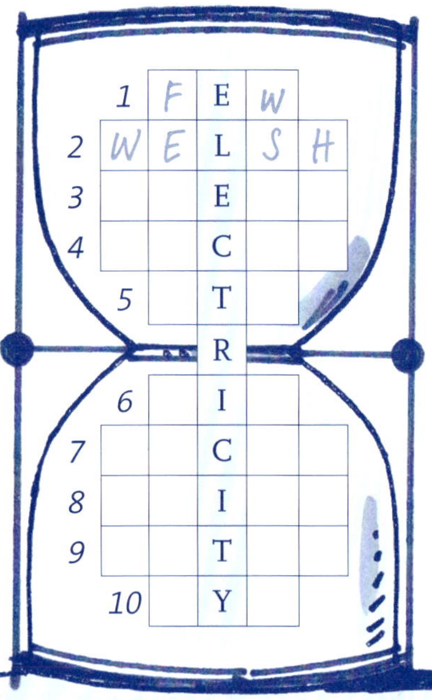

1 ein paar/einige – Spaß
2 Geld – walisisch
3 heute – sauber
4 Feind – Tatsachen
5 aß – Arm
6 Mülltonne – Kunst
7 Löffel – Schinkenspeck
8 Rock – Flöte
9 nachdem – sonnig
10 hinzufügen – Auge

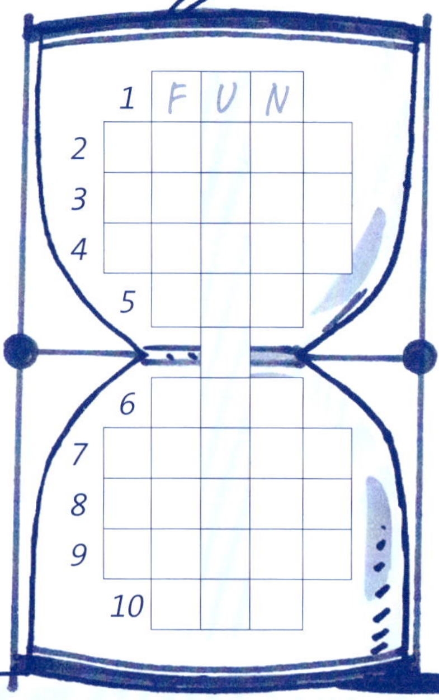

Das geheime Wort in der rechten Sanduhr heißt: Englisch ______________________

Deutsch ______________________

17 Picture puzzle

Vergleiche die beiden Bilder miteinander. Welche 8 Gegenstände fehlen auf dem rechten Bild?

a purse ______________________ ______________________

______________________ ______________________

______________________ ______________________

______________________ ______________________

New words ▸ pp. 30–31

eine **riesige** Party mit über 250 Gästen	a ______ party with more than 250 guests
Ein **Lachs** ist ein großer Fisch.	A ______ is a big fish.
die schöne Landschaft **genießen**	enjoy the beautiful ______

1 Word friends

Welche Wörter aus den Kieselsteinen passen in die Lücken?

listen – wait – become – ~~eat~~ – know – speak – dream – read – do – keep

1 eat salmon / a huge meal / too much
2 ______ for a bus / for ages / outside
3 ______ of the future / that you can fly
4 ______ a good book / and write / instructions
5 ______ two languages / more slowly / to me
6 ______ to the radio / for the doorbell
7 ______ all the answers / lots of people
8 ______ a gig / your homework / judo
9 ______ a teacher / tired / very excited
10 ______ in touch / the window open

2 Words with different meanings

Finde in der Liste die passenden Wörter zu den Paaren 1–7. Trage sie ein und unterstreiche die deutschen Entsprechungen.

1
a) Wie ist dein Name?
b) Kannst du die Hauptstadt von Schottland nennen?
______

2
a) Die Speisekarte liegt auf dem Tisch.
b) Klicke mit der Maus auf das Menü.
______

3
a) Vergiss nicht das Wechselgeld.
b) Wo müssen wir umsteigen?
______

4
a) Ist er ledig oder verheiratet?
b) eine einfache Fahrkarte kaufen
single

5
a) Das Gegenteil von *groß* ist *klein*.
b) Gegenüber dem Kino gibt es ein Café.
______

6
a) Meine Eltern arbeiten in einer Fabrik.
b) Die Fahrstühle waren kaputt, aber jetzt funktionieren sie wieder.
______

7
a) ein gepflegter Garten
b) eine tolle Idee
______

8
a) Lass uns zu Fuß gehen!
b) einen Spaziergang machen
______

change
neat
menu
name
opposite
~~single~~
work
walk

New words ▸ p. 32

Meine Eltern mögen keine **elektronische** Musik.	My parents don't like ________ music.
die neuen **Medien** wie das Internet oder E-Mail	the new ________ like the internet or e-mail
eine **abgelegene** Insel besuchen	visit a ________________ island
Mein **Urgroßvater** wird dieses Jahr 90 Jahre alt.	My __________________ will be 90 this year.
Ich hatte nicht viel **Post** – nur einen Brief.	I didn't have much ________ – only one letter.
Hast du ihn nur **einmal** gesehen?	Did you only see him ______ ?
Das Boot kommt **zweimal pro** Woche	The Boat comes ________________ a week.
Stell dir vor, du bist eine Katze.	________________ you're a cat.
Filme auf DVD für den **Gebrauch** im Unterricht	films on DVD for ____________ in lessons
Bücher mit anderen Schülern **austauschen**	____________ books with other students
Ich habe einen neuen **Klingelton** für mein Handy.	I've got a new ____________ for my mobile.
Wir können diese zwei Lieder **mischen**.	We can ________ these two songs.

3 Number crossword

Gleiche Zahlen sind gleiche Buchstaben.
Die angegebenen Lösungen helfen dir,
das gesamte Rätsel zu lösen.
Alle Wörter sind in dieser Unit neu.

Wo im Rätsel findet man das englische Wort für ...

1 elektronisch e down
2 riesig j across
3 zweimal ____________
4 einmal ____________
5 Medien ____________
6 austauschen ____________
7 sich (etwas) vorstellen ____________
8 Landschaft ____________

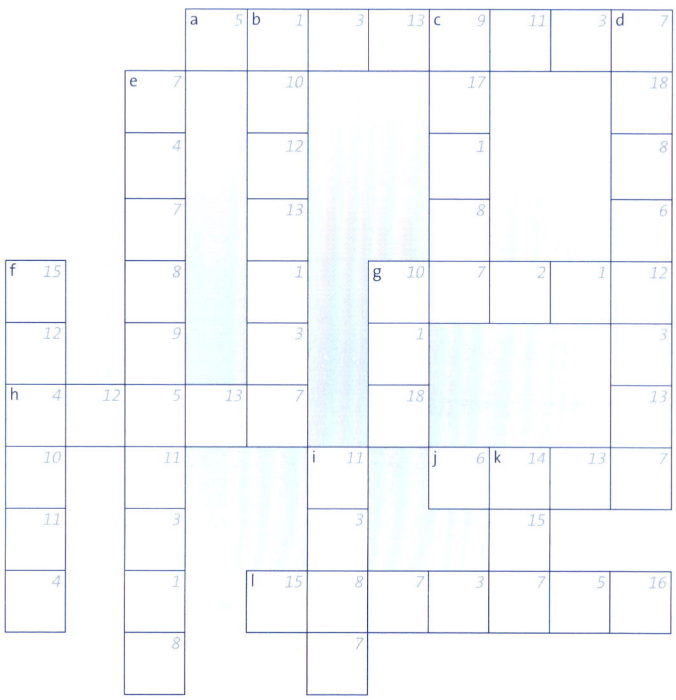

New words ▸ p. 33

Ich kann dich am Flughafen **abholen**.	I can _______ you _______ at the airport.
Wieviele Schüler gehen aufs **Gymnasium**?	How many students go to _______________ ?
Er arbeitet als **Rechercheur** fürs Fernsehen.	He works as a TV _______________ .
die **Schönheit** der Berge Schottlands	the _______________ of Scotland's mountains
einen **schicken** Pullover tragen	wear a _______________ pullover
Wie lange **dauert** der Flug nach Berlin?	How long does the flight to Berlin _________ ?
Der Laden ist geöffnet **von** Montag **bis** Sonnabend.	The shop opens _______ Monday ___ Saturday.
Öffnet das Schwimmbad **während** des Winters?	Does the pool open ____________ the winter?
Er war **überrascht**, als ich plötzlich hineinkam.	He was __________ when I suddenly came in.
Sag kein Wort! Wir wollen Vati **überraschen**.	Don't say a word! We want to __________ dad.
Welche **Rolle** möchtest du spielen?	Which __________ do you want to play?

4 Scrambled words: school

Löse die Buchstabenrätsel, um Wörter zu finden, die mit Schule zusammenhängen. Trage die deutschen Übersetzungen ein. Die markierten Buchstaben ergeben das „geheime Wort".

1 Teal Bit Em T I M E T A B L E Stundenplan

2 Trace Eh _ _ _ _ _ _ _ ______________

3 Cam Tassel _ _ _ _ _ _ _ _ _ ______________

4 Hay Idols _ _ _ _ _ _ _ _ ______________

5 Bad Or _ _ _ _ _ ______________

6 Sic Enec _ _ _ _ _ _ _ ______________

5 Spot the mistakes

In jedem Satz sind zwei Fehler. Unterstreiche und korrigiere sie. Es gibt Rechtschreib- und grammatische Fehler.

1 Hoy is one of the biger Orkney ilands. bigger ________

2 Live on an iceland can be boring sometimes. ________ ________

3 Katrina have a mobil, so she often texts her friends. ________ ________

4 She also write e-mails once or twice a weak. ________ ________

5 She sometimes downloads musik from a webseite. ________ ________

6 Word groups

Übersetze die deutschen Wörter auf den Zetteln ins Englische und füge sie in die richtige Wortgruppe ein.

pets	media	transport
dog		

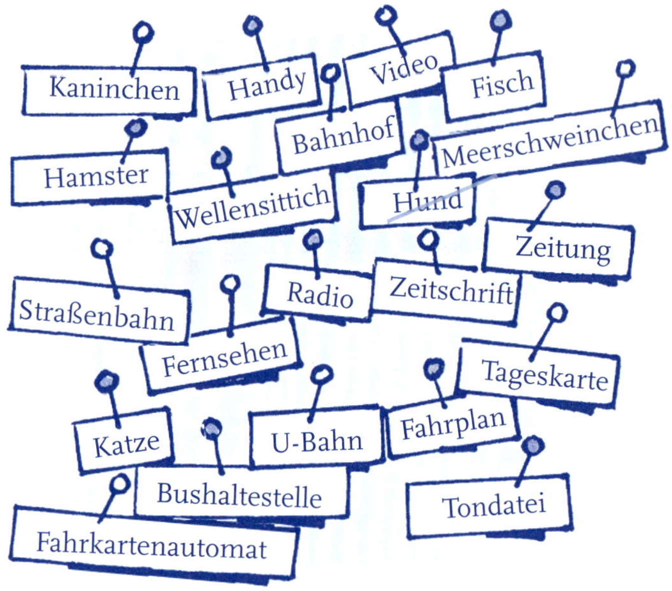

7 Making phrases

Vervollständige die Ausdrücke mit dem Verb vom richtigen Zettel.

1 take ______ a photo of the cows in the field

2 ______ a text message to a friend

3 ______ the arrival times in the timetable

4 ______ all the hungry farm animals

5 ______ the train at the next station

6 ______ your mum on your mobile

7 ______ at the bus stop

8 ______ a sound file from the Internet

8 Opposites

Trage die Gegenteile der fett gedruckten Wörter in die Lücken ein.

1 **crowded** / empty streets

2 The film had a strange **beginning** / ______ .

3 **remember** / ______ a name

4 an **unimportant** / ______ detail

5 She's **friendly** / ______ to everyone.

6 a **wet** / ______ towel

7 at the **back** / ______ of the room

8 I really love **spicy** / ______ food.

9 take the **northbound** / ______ train

10 buy a **cheap** /an ______ pullover

11 do something for the **first** / ______ time

12 We saw the **king** / ______ on TV.

New words ▸ *p. 34*

Diesmal gewinne ich! – **Das hättest du wohl gern**!	This time I'm going to win. – ______________ !
Ist dir kalt? **Soll ich** das Fenster schließen?	Are you cold? ____________ close the window?
Wir mussten einen großen **Rucksack** packen.	We had to pack a big ______________ .
Ihre Haare sind zu kurz für einen **Pferdeschwanz**.	Her hair is too short for a ________________ .

9 What are the words?

Welches Wort passt besser in die Lücken: **able** *oder* **allowed**?

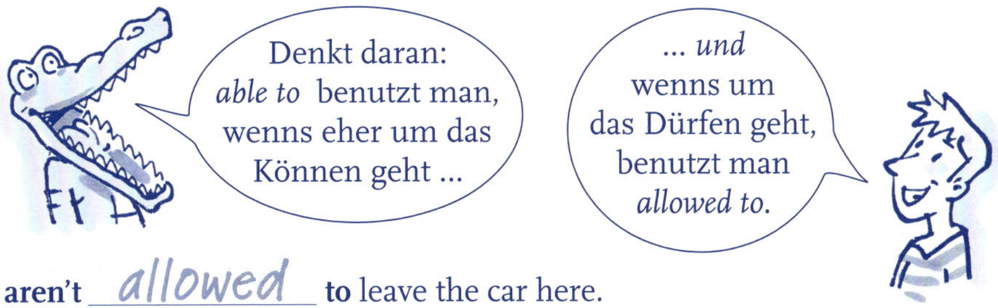

1 Mum! Look at the sign. You **aren't** allowed **to** leave the car here.

2 The homework was so difficult. Even Dad **wasn't** ____________ **to** help me with it.

3 Dilek's very good at languages. She's ____________ **to** speak German, Turkish and English.

4 **Are** we ____________ **to** cycle in the park? – No, we aren't. The sign says 'No bikes'.

5 Sorry, I won't **be** ____________ **to** meet you later. I just haven't got enough time.

6 **I'm** ____________ **to** stay up late at weekends, but I have to go to bed at 9 on weekdays.

10 Word pairs

Welche Wörter passen zusammen?

New words ▸ p. 35

Ich bin **gekränkt**, weil du unhöflich zu mir warst.	I'm ______________ because you were rude to me.
Es **kränkt** mich, wenn du unhöflich bist.	It ______________ me when you're rude.
Mutti **erlaubt** mir nicht, Make-up zu tragen.	Mum doesn't ____________ me wear make-up.
Leider gibt's an jeder Schule einen **Schultyrannen**.	I'm afraid there's a ____________ at every school.
Er **hat** mir wieder **Schimpfwörter nachgerufen**.	He ______________ me ____________ again.
Sie **tratschen** die ganze Zeit über Jungs.	They ______________ about boys all the time.
Wir sind zu spät. Ich **wette**, wir verpassen den Bus.	We're late. I ______________ we'll miss the bus.
Vergiss nicht abzuschließen, wenn du gehst.	Don't ______________ to lock up when you go.
die **Haupt**informationen finden	find the ___________________ information
Ich wollte nicht deine **Gefühle** verletzen.	I didn't want to hurt your ___________________ .
Was ist die **Übersetzung** dieses Wortes?	What's the ___________________ of this word?
Kannst du dieses Wort ins Deutsche **übersetzen**?	Can you ______________ this word into German?

11 Lost words

Die fehlenden Wörter stecken im Maul des Hais.
Finde sie und ergänze die Sätze.

1 The water here can be dangerous, so it's unsafe to go swimming.

2 It's ________________ to eat fruit and vegetables every day.

3 Jane's room is always in a mess – she's so ________________ !

4 I think it's ________________ if you don't do any sport.

5 Sue never laughs or smiles. She can't be a very ________________ person.

6 Which of you knows the ________________ answer?

7 I'm ________________ to hear you aren't feeling well.

8 Sorry, but I'm not ________________ if I can come to your party on Saturday.

9 Jo was very ________________ when he lost his favourite earring.

10 I was ________________ about the meaning, so I looked the word up.

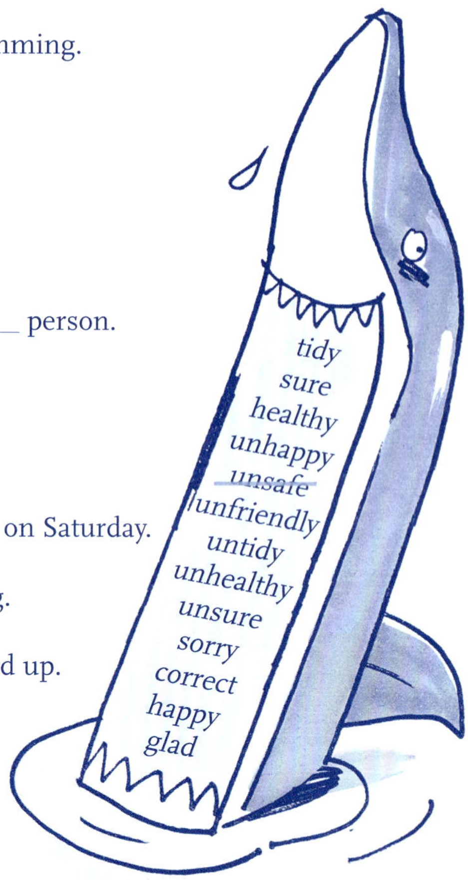

New words ▸ pp. 38 – 43

Die **Betonung** liegt auf der dritten Silbe.	The __________ is on the third syllable.
Du **hattest Glück**, dass du das Geld gefunden hast.	You ________________ to find the money.
Es ist nicht einfach, einen **Kreis** zu zeichnen.	It's not easy to draw a ______________ .
Was war der **Höhepunkt** unseres Ausflugs?	What was the ____________ of our trip?
Das Schloss ist ein **beeindruckendes** Gebäude.	The castle is an ________________ building.
Dein Aufsatz braucht eine bessere **Gliederung**.	Your essay needs a better ______________ .
Wir haben den **Anfang** des Films verpasst.	We missed the ________________ of the film.
eine **allgemeine** Erklärung ohne viele Details	a __________ explanation without many details
Es ist **persönlich**. Ich will nicht darüber reden.	It's __________ . I don't want to talk about it.
ein paar **Souvenirs** aus meinem Urlaub	a few ________________ from my holiday
Ich mag keine langen **Zugreisen**.	I don't like long train ________________ .
Die Touristen lieben die schottischen **Seen**.	Tourists like the Scottish ______________ .
Der See ist 14 **Kilometer** lang.	The lake ist 14 __________ long.
Wieviele **Zentimeter** hat ein Meter?	How many __________ are there in a metre?
Millionen Menschen sahen diesen Film.	________________ people saw this film.

12 The fourth word

Welches Wort fehlt hier?

1 one – two	once – ________________
2 good – bad	intelligent – ____________
3 central – centre	beautiful – _____________
4 build – building	fly – __________________
5 ride – ridden	forget – ______________
6 describe – description	begin – _______________
7 invite – invitation	translate – ____________
8 husband – wife	husbands – ____________
9 spoon – spoons	knife – _______________

13 Odd word out

Unterstreiche das Wort, das nicht passt.

1 car – bay – bus – bike

2 essay – felt tip – pen – pencil

3 danger – teacher – butcher – engineer

4 onion – mushroom – sausages – pea

5 harbour – ferry – boat – ship

6 tired – hungry – thirsty – sleep

7 first – twice – third – fourth

8 east – left – north – south

9 mail – join – text – phone

14 More about: Orkney

Vervollständige den Text mit Wörtern vom Ticket.

ORKNEY TICKET
and
another
between
biggest
but
for
history
~~islands~~
make
on
takes
under

Orkney is a group of islands (1) ten miles from the Scottish coast. Today, about 20,000 people live ________ (2) 17 of the 70 islands. Most – about 15,000 – live on the ________ (3) island, Mainland. Between five ________ (4) 550 people live on the other islands. Hoy, the second largest island, has just under 300 people.

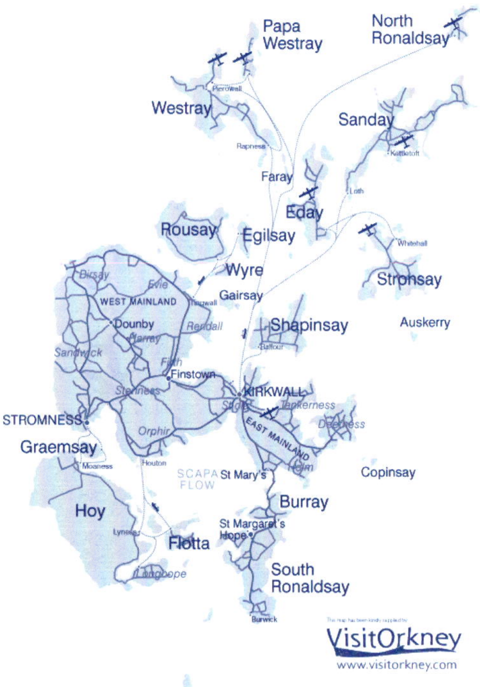

Orkney hasn't got many people, ________ (5) it has lots of schools – 21 for about 3,300 students. Some of the schools are very small – four of them have ________ (6) ten students.

When people travel from one island to ________ (7) they go by ferry, or fly between the bigger islands. The shortest flight is ________ (8) Westray and Papa Westray – it ________ (9) only two minutes. Orkney is great ________ (10) holidays. If you go there, you can stay on a farm and learn how to ________ (11) cheese, enjoy the clean air and beautiful beaches and find out more about the 5,500 year ________ (12) of the people on the islands.

15 The best word

Finde das Wort in der Strickleiter, das am besten in die Lücke passt.

busy	excited
~~exciting~~	hilly
personal	realistic
royal	strange
special	spicy
large	upset
correct	huge
mild	personal
friendly	realistic
central	uncool
central	huge
realistic	stupid
busy	surprising
lovely	surprised

1 Here's some exciting news. Mum's going to have another baby!

2 Open a window please. There's a ________ smell in the room.

3 Kim was very ________ because nobody came to visit her.

4 They live in a ________ house with 17 bedrooms.

5 Nobody likes Angela. She's so ________ !

6 Fantastic! That's a very ________ plan.

7 I was ________ when I saw Peter. I thought he was abroad.

New words ▸ *pp. 45 – 46*

Und jetzt zu einem anderen Thema.	____________ another topic.
Achte auf **Durchsagen** im Bahnhof.	Listen for ____________ at the station.
Er ist **Schulleiter** einer großen Schule.	He's the ____________ of a big school.
Das kann nicht wahr sein – ich **glaube** es nicht.	That can't be true – I don't ____________ it.
Du bist der Sieger! **Herzlichen Glückwunsch**!	You're the winner! ____________ !
Es **könnte vielleicht** regnen – hast du eine Jacke?	It ____________ rain – have you got a jacket?
Welcher **Friseur** schneidet dir die Haare?	Which ____________ cuts your hair?
Er war **schockiert**, als er die Nachricht hörte.	He was ____________ when he heard the news.
Er weiß, **was er tun soll**, wenn es ein Problem gibt.	He knows ____________ if there's a problem.
Sie rannte schnell über die Straße **hinüber**.	She ran quickly ____________ the road.
Dieser **Anorak** ist schön warm.	This ____________ is nice and warm.
Sie **necken** mich, weil ich komische Ohren habe.	They ____________ me because I have funny ears.
Wir warteten drinnen, **bis** der Regen aufhörte.	We waited inside ____________ the rain stopped.
Lass uns **vorne** im Bus sitzen.	Let's sit ____________ of the bus.
Der **Kapitän** begrüßte die **Passagiere**.	The ____________ welcomed the ____________ .
Ich hole dich ab – wann ist deine **Ankunfts**zeit?	I'll pick you up – what's your ____________ time?
am **Kai** auf ein Schiff warten	wait for a ship on the ____________

16 Last letter – first letter

Der letzte Buchstabe von jedem Wort ist gleichzeitig der erste des nächsten Wortes.

1 Stundenplan
2 aufgeregt
3 Detektiv
4 Elefant
5 dauern/(Zeit) brauchen
6 Aufzug
7 Fels
8 Schlüssel
9 du/ihr/dir/euch
10 bis
11 schön
12 gähnen

New words ▸ pp. 47–48

Die Diebe kamen, **während** wir weg waren.	The thieves came __________ we were out.
Welche **Ausrüstung** braucht man für Judo?	What ______________ do you need for judo?
Es ging schnell – es war **im Nu** vorbei.	It was quick – it was over ________________ .
Sein Name **steht über** seiner Adresse und	His name is ______________ his address and
... seine Telefonnummer ist **unter** der Adresse.	... his phone number is __________ the address.
Das Auto **raste** die Straße entlang.	The car ______________ along the street.
Er **baute** die Kamera **auf** und fing an zu filmen.	He _____ the camera _____ and started to film.
Klippen sind gefährlich –man kann leicht stürzen.	_______ are dangerous – you can easily fall.
Ich brauche Fleisch und Gemüse für den **Eintopf**.	I need meat and vegetables for the __________ .
Die meisten Dörfer haben eine **Gemeindehalle**.	Most villages have a ______________________ .
Der Dieb **schnappte** mein Handy und rannte weg.	The thief ___________ my mobile and ran away.
Wir **trauten** unseren **Augen kaum**.	We ______________________ our ________ .

17 Word search: town and country

Im Rätsel sind 16 „town and country"-Wörter versteckt. Finde sie und übersetze sie ins Deutsche. (↓ →)

hill – Hügel ________________

________________ ________________

________________ ________________

________________ ________________

________________ ________________

________________ ________________

________________ ________________

________________ ________________

A	G	H	I	L	L	R	O	A	D
I	I	F	F	Y	B	A	Y	M	M
U	S	A	B	E	A	C	H	O	J
C	L	R	H	A	R	B	O	U	R
A	A	M	S	E	A	F	C	N	S
S	N	C	L	W	P	I	A	T	Q
T	D	O	A	B	D	E	N	A	U
L	H	A	K	J	U	L	A	I	A
E	B	S	E	B	Q	D	L	N	R
L	Y	T	O	W	E	R	L	X	E

16 Vocabulary network

Vervollständige das Wörternetz.
Die Verben, die auf den Zetteln fehlen, bringt der Geier.
Die anderen Wörter findest du im Sand.

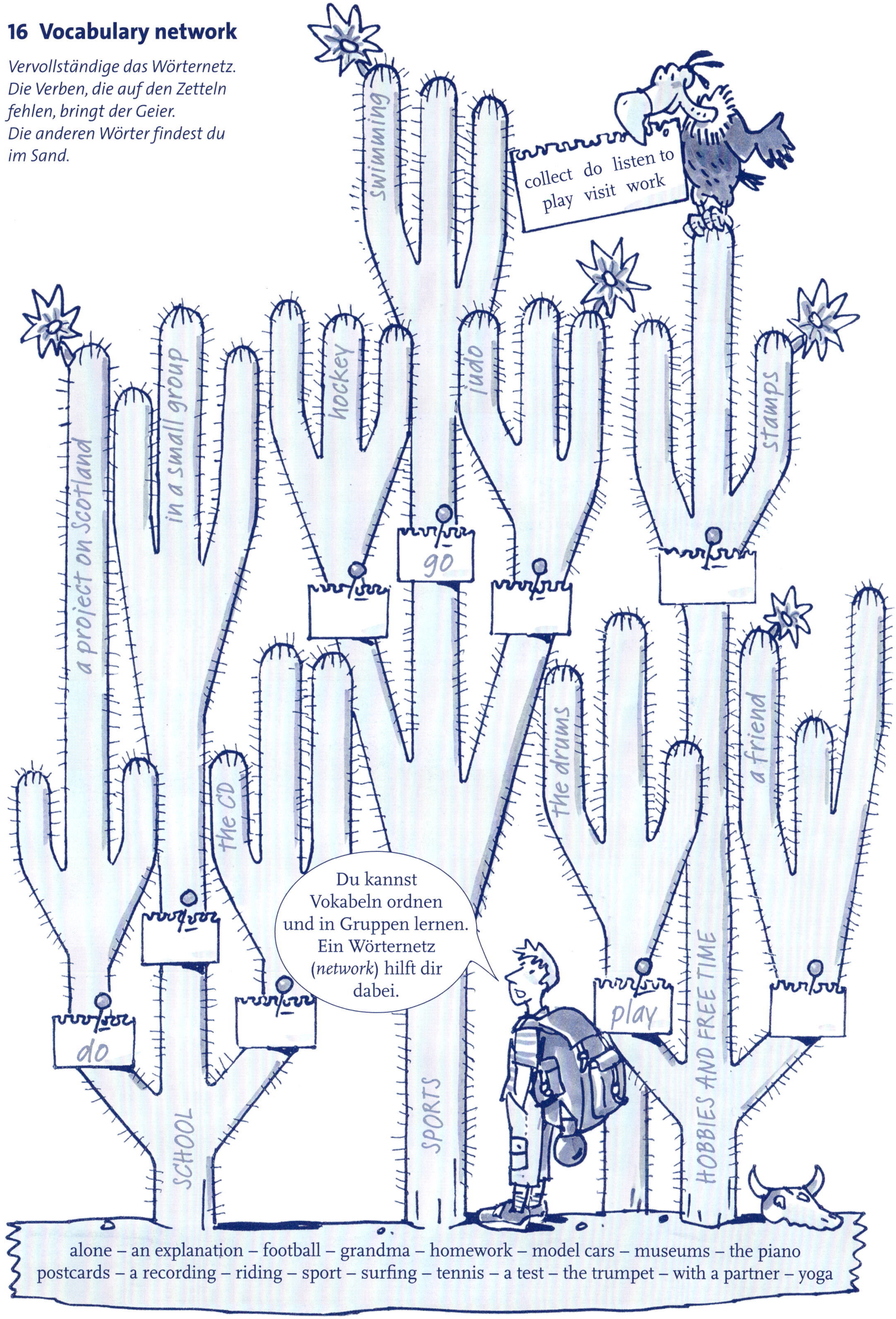

Unit 3

New words ▸ pp. 54–55

Hast du wirklich Karten für das **Endspiel**?	Have you really got tickets for the __________ ?
Leider wird dies sein **letztes** Spiel sein.	I'm afraid this will be his __________ game.
Er gewann das **Halbfinale**, verlor aber das Endspiel.	He won the __________ , but lost the final.
eine **Trainingseinheit** verpassen	miss a __________
In unserem Verein **trainieren** wir jeden Montag.	In our club we __________ every Monday.
Eine große Wohnung braucht viele **Möbel**.	A big flat needs lots of __________ .

1 What are the words?

Finde für jeden Satz ein passendes deutsches Wort. Übersetze es und setze es ein. Wähle dann die richtige Form des Verbs **be**.

Nicht vergessen!
Es gibt Wörter, die im Deutschen Plural sein können, im Englischen aber immer Einzahl sind.

Beweise · Verkehrsmittel · Nachrichten · Möbel · Hausaufgaben · ~~Informationen~~ · Haare

1 All the information about Manchester is in the brochure. (is/are)

2 Yesterday's Maths __________ __________ so hard – I wasn't able to do it all. (were/was)

3 What colour __________ Latisha's __________ ? Black or dark brown? (are/is)

4 __________ here __________ very good. The buses are always late. (isn't/aren't)

5 There __________ a lot of __________ in the room – only a few chairs. (weren't/wasn't)

6 What time __________ the next __________ on TV? (is/are)

7 __________ there any __________ that there's life on other planets? (is/are)

2 The fourth word

Welches Wort wird hier gesucht?

1 one – two / once – __________

2 plane – airport / ship – __________

3 woodpecker – bird / salmon – __________

4 banana – fruit / pea – __________

5 school – head teacher / ship – __________

6 January – month / winter – __________

7 bread – food / armchair – __________

8 rain – fall / sun – __________

9 cathedral – building / trumpet – __________

10 lunch – meal / stew – __________

3 Hidden words

Ergänze die Wortgruppen, indem du Wörter mit Buchstaben der Wörter ***„training session“*** *bildest.*

4 Word families

a) Finde die passenden Verben zu den angegebenen Nomen.

1 arrival – arrive
2 beginning – ___________
3 explanation – ___________
4 feeling – ___________
5 meaning – ___________
6 mixture – ___________
7 movement – ___________
8 murder – ___________
9 phone – ___________
10 practice – ___________
11 bully – ___________
12 invitation – ___________
13 teacher – ___________
14 translation – ___________

b) Vervollständige die Sätze mit einem Nomen oder einem Verb aus der Liste in a).

1 What's the meaning of this word? Can you ______________ it please?

2 I've got an ______________ to Dan's party. – Really? Do you think he'll ______________ me too?

3 How often do you ______________ the piano?

4 Please ______________ me and tell me when you ______________ at the station.

5 I read the book in English, but my little brother read the German ______________ .

New words ▸ pp. 56–57

Unsere **Anhänger** kommen zu jedem Spiel.	Our ____________ come to every match.
Viele Jugendliche **unterstützen** die Mannschaft.	Lots of teenagers ____________ the team.
Wir hatten **so** schönes Wetter – jeden Tag Sonne.	We had ________ nice weather – sun every day.
Die Fans jubelten, als Black ein **Tor schoss**.	The fans cheered when Black ____________ .
Nach 45 Minuten war der **Spielstand** 2:1.	After 45 minutes the ____________ was 2–1
Der Ball sah gut aus, aber er flog am **Tor** vorbei.	The ball looked good, but it flew past the _____ .
Ist der **Trainer** böse auf seine Spieler?	Is the ____________ angry with his players?
Musik ist zum Tanzen da.	____________________________ .
Dein neuer **Gymnastikanzug** sieht sehr schön aus!	Your new ____________ looks great!
Passt die blaue **Strumpfhose** zu roten Schuhen?	Do the blue ____________ go with red shoes?
Mein **Ziel** im Leben ist, glücklich zu sein.	My ________ in life is to be happy.
Es sieht schlecht aus: es gibt fast keine **Hoffnung**.	It's looking bad: there's almost no ________ .
ein deutscher **Austauschschüler** in England	a German ____________ student in England
Ideen mit anderen Schülern **austauschen**	____________ ideas with other students
Ich war nicht da, als er kam. – **Schlechtes Timing!**	I was out when he came. – ____________ !
Hungrig? – Nein, ich habe keinen **Appetit**.	Hungry? – No, I've got no ____________ .
versuchen, einen Satz zu **umschreiben**	try to ________________ a sentence

5 Word friends

In jedem Haus gibt es drei Wörter bzw. Wortverbindungen, die man direkt nach dem Verb auf der Fahne benutzen kann. Unterstreiche sie.

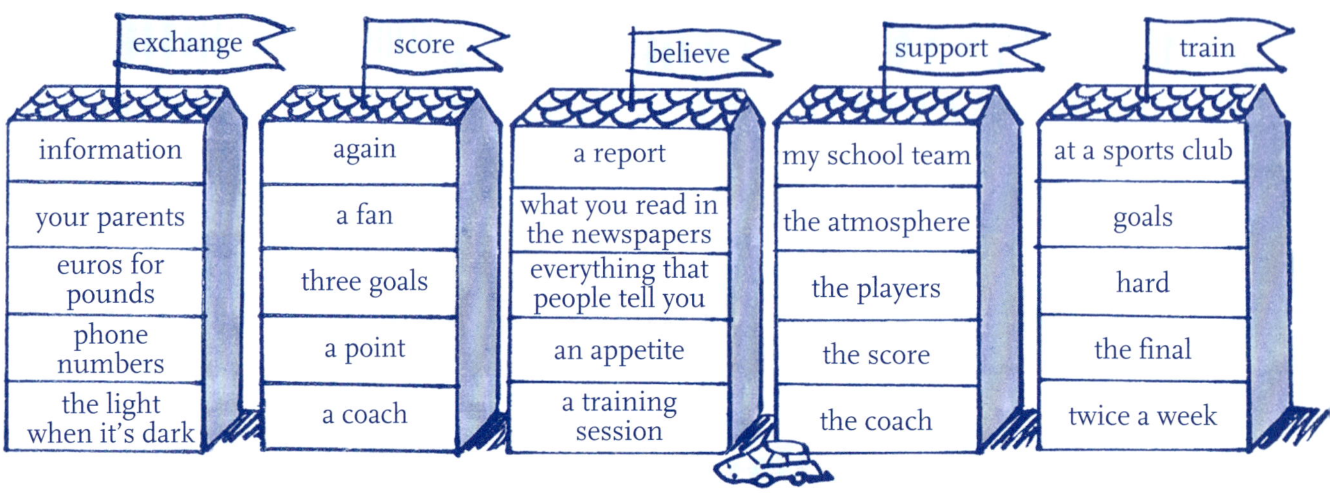

6 Words in pictures

a) Trage die angezeigten Körperteile ein.

1 face ______ 6 ______

2 ______ 7 ______

3 ______ 8 ______

4 ______ 9 ______

5 ______

b) Unterstreiche die beiden Wörter, die am besten zu den fettgedruckten Wörtern passen.

1 a broken / pretty / round **face**

2 blue / bright / loud **eyes**

3 a long / small / tidy **nose**

4 my left / medium / right **ear**

5 broken / careful / white **teeth**

6 grey / slow / tidy **hair**

7 a big / early / loud **mouth**

8 cheap / clean / strong **hands**

7 Definitions

Vervollständige die Definitionen mit Wörtern aus den Mauersteinen. Trage die richtigen Wörter aus der Sprühwolke in die rechte Spalte ein.

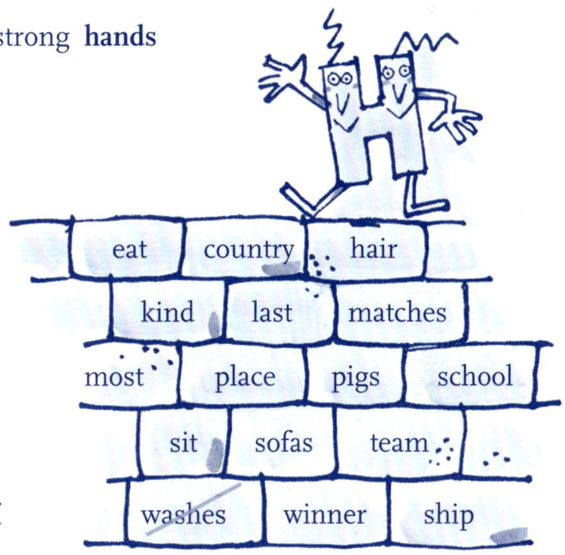

1 a person who washes and cuts other people's ______ hairdresser

2 a ______ of hotel where you can ______ or sleep cheaply ______

3 a person who likes a ______, wears the team's colours, goes to ______ ______

4 the ______ match – the ______ is the champion ______

5 things like chairs or ______ where you can ______ or lie down ______

6 the ______ important teacher at a ______ ______

7 a person who works in the ______, often with cows, ______ etc. ______

8 the ______ at a harbour where you get on (or off) a ______ ______

New words ▸ pp. 58–59

Lass uns **eine Abmachung treffen**.	Let's ______________ .
Hol die Taschen – es ist Zeit, das Auto zu **beladen**.	Get the bags – it's time to ______________ the car.
Helft mir, die Taschen aus dem Auto zu **entladen**!	Help me to ______________ the bags from the car.
die **Gemälde** in einer **Galerie** sehen	see the ______________ in a ______________
an einem **Wettbewerb** teilnehmen und gewinnen	take part in a ______________ and win
Einsendungen an diese Adresse bis zum 30. Mai!	______________ to this address by 30th May!
Wann hast du diesen Brief **empfangen**?	When did you ______________ this letter?
Wann werden Sie die Gewinner **bekanntgeben**?	When will they ______________ the winners?
Können wir diese Mannschaft **schlagen**?	Can we ______________ this team?
Ich hoffe, diese E-Mail **erreicht** dich.	I hope this e-mail ______________ you.
Es war ein fantastischer **Sieg** über United.	It was a fantastic ______________ against United.
Spitzenspieler verdienen viel Geld.	______________ players earn lots of money.
Er spielt in der **Verteidigung**, aber schießt oft Tore.	He plays in ______________ , but often scores.
Der Spielstand in der **Halbzeit** war 2:1.	The score at ______________ was 2–1.
Nach sechs Minuten **gingen wir in Führung**.	We ______________ after six minutes.
Wer wird den **Strafstoß** schießen?	Who is going to take the ______________ ?
Der **Torwart** hat den Ball gehalten,	The ______________ held the ball
... obwohl es ein toller **Schuss** war.	... although it was a great ______________ .

8 Verb forms

Ergänze die Tabelle der unregelmäßigen Verben.

1	do	did	done
2		grew	
3		took	
4	win		
5		lost	
6			beaten
7		chose	

8	begin		
9		rode	
10			cut
11			forgotten
12		let	
13	upset		
14			caught

9 Last letter – first letter

Der letzte Buchstabe von jedem Wort ist gleichzeitig der erste des nächsten Wortes.

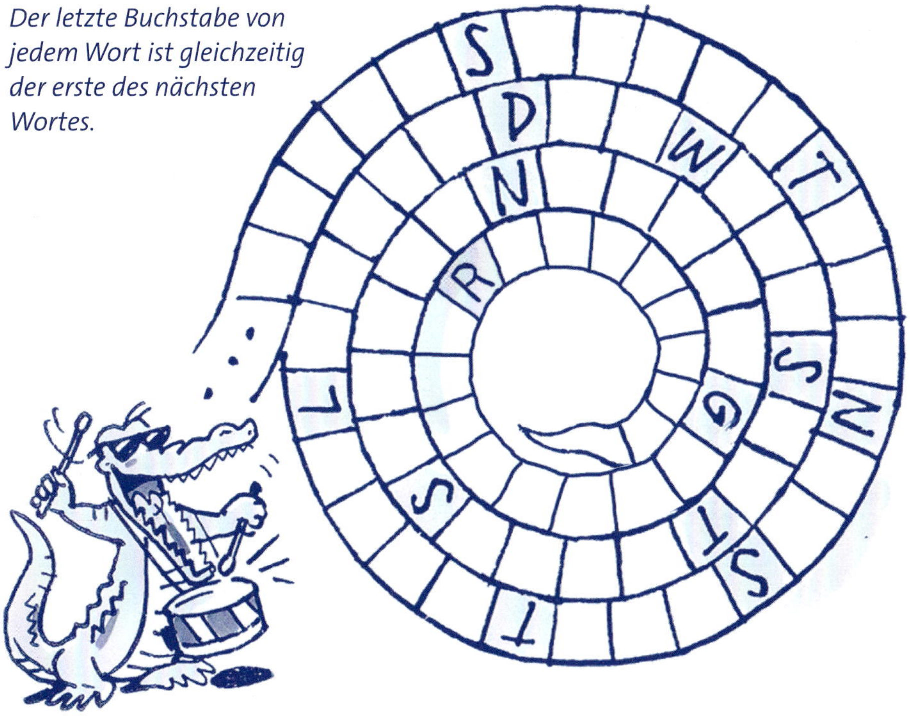

1 Betonung
2 unterstützen
3 trainieren
4 Nachrichten
5 Hemd
6 reisen
7 Gymnastikanzug
8 Unentschieden
9 Wörter
10 Schuss
11 Strumpfhose
12 Bahnhof
13 nichts
14 Torwart
15 wirklichkeitsnah

10 Pronunciation

Ordne die Wörter aus der Box der richtigen Aussprachegruppe zu.

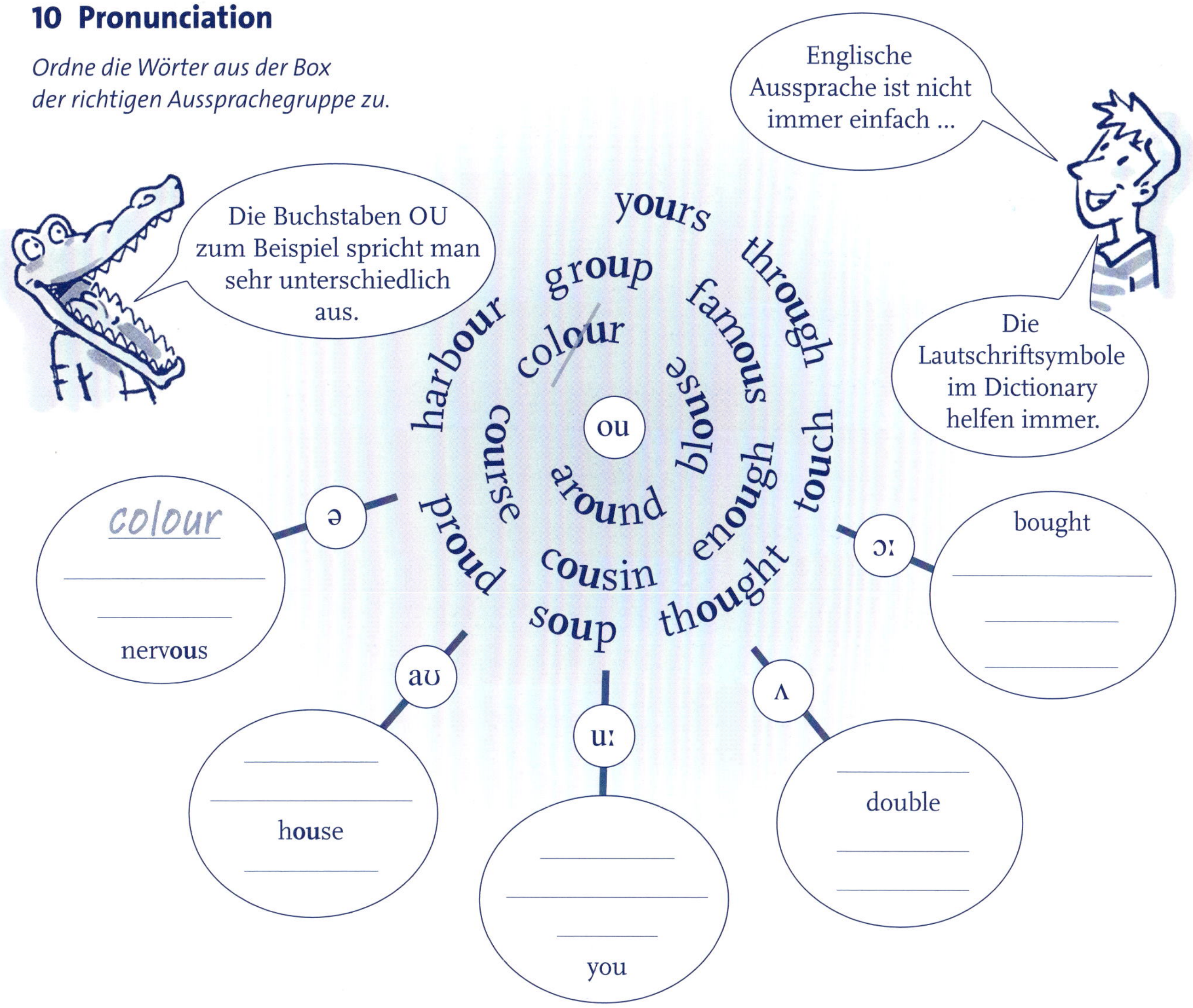

New words ▸ pp. 60–65

Wenn du einen Fehler **entdeckst**, korrigiere ihn.	When you ______________ a mistake, correct it.
der **Unterschied** zwischen Stadt und Land	the ______________ between town and country
zwei **Stimmen** gegen den Plan und 50 dafür	two ______________ against the plan and 50 for it
den **Pokal** im Endspiel gewinnen	win the ______________ in the final
Das Feuer **zerstörte** den alten Turm.	The fire ____________________ the old tower.
Er arbeitet in der Lebensmittel**industrie**.	He works in the food ____________________ .
Deutschland ist ein **Industrie**land.	Germany is an ____________________ country.
einen Zeitschriftenartiikel über **Prominente** lesen	read a magazine article about _________________
Ausflüge zu Fußball**stadien organisieren**	_________________ trips to football ______________
ein **Ausgleichstor** in der 90. Minute **erzielen**	____________________ in the 90th minute
einen schlechten **Schiedsrichter ersetzen**	____________________ a bad ____________________
Ich tanze **ab und zu**, aber nicht jede Woche.	I dance ______________ , but not every week.
Schreibe einige Sätze **über dich selbst**.	Write some sentences _______________________ .

11 Word ladder

Gehe von unten nach oben, indem du bei jeder Sprosse einen Buchstaben veränderst.

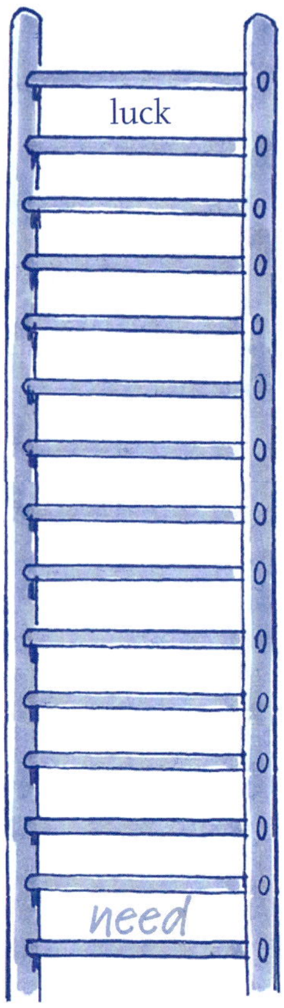

Good ★ in your English test tomorrow.
Please close the windows and ★ up before you leave.
I can't find my key. Can you help me ★ for it?
prepare hot meals
I ★ some photos with my new camera yesterday.
How many pages are there in that ★?
The English word for 'Fußballschuh' is football ★.
You can travel on water with this.
Manchester United ★ Bayern Munich 2–1.
No sausages for me, please. I never eat ★.
Let's ★ tomorrow at 4 o'clock.
one foot – two ★
give food to an animal or person
The show is free, so we don't ★ any tickets.

12 More about ... Manchester United

Vervollständige den Text mit den Wörtern aus der Box.

club even huge learn
match millions over rich
players third than times

Manchester United is a famous English football club (1). They've been football champions of England 16 __________ (2) and, in 1968, they were the first English club to win the European Cup. In 2008 they won it a __________ (3) time. ManU isn't just popular in England. All __________ (4) the world, the club has __________ (5) of supporters. And it is very __________ (6), so it has enough money to buy the best __________ (7) (like Wayne Rooney or Cristiano Ronaldo). ManU's home is the __________ (8) stadium at Old Trafford, with room for 75,000 fans to watch a __________ (9) . The club has __________ (10) got a museum. More __________ (11) 200,000 visitors go there every year to __________ (12) about ManU's great past.

13 Hour glasses

Übersetze die Wörter und trage sie in die passende Sanduhr ein.

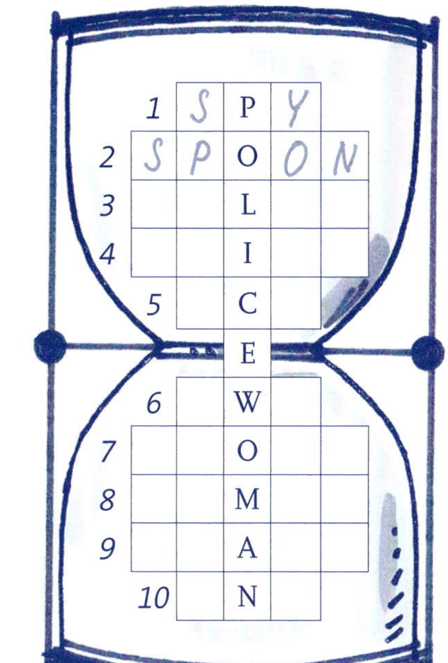

1 ~~wer~~ – Spion
2 Trainer – Löffel
3 Lineal –Preis, Gewinn
4 sich beeilen – Hemd
5 Eis – hinzufügen
6 Kugelschreiber – zwei
7 gekränkt – Spielstand
8 Aufsatz – römisch
9 Stahl – Zug
10 Schluss – Kunst

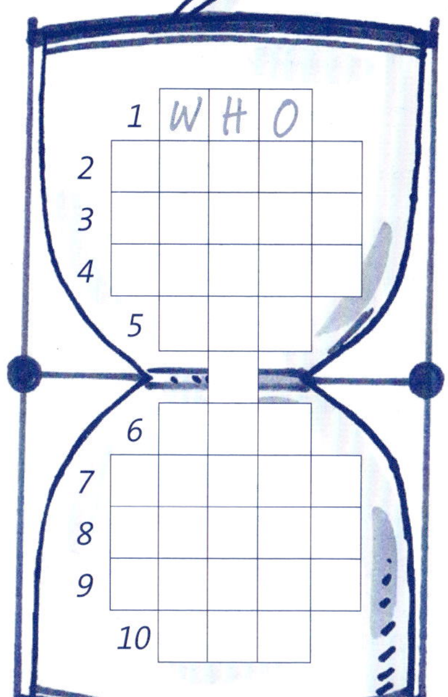

Das geheime Wort heißt: Englisch __________________

Deutsch __________________

New words ▸ pp. 69–70

Sogar im Sommer ist es kalt hier.	It's cold here ____________ in the summer.
Papa **ist** in einer großen Familie **aufgewachsen**.	Dad ____________________ in a big family.
Jack schob den Rollstuhl **auf** die Fähre.	Jack pushed the wheelchair __________ the ferry.
Lass uns eine Boots**fahrt** auf dem See **machen**.	Let's _______ a boat __________ on the lake.
Ein Unfall! Ruf einen **Krankenwagen**!	An accident! Call an ____________________ !
Er hat eine **Medaille** in **Leichtathletik** gewonnen.	He won a __________ in _______________ .
Schnee! Nun kann ich meinen **Schlitten** benutzen.	Snow! Now I can use my __________ !
Spielt Schottland in der **Meisterschaft**?	Is Scotland playing in the _______________ ?
Die Spieler mussten hart **um** den Titel **kämpfen**.	The players had to _______ hard _____ the title.
Die **Operation** hat ihm das Leben gerettet.	The ____________________ saved his life.
Sind diese Blumen **künstlich** oder echt?	Are these flowers _______________ or real?
Ich habe einen Rollstuhl, weil ich **behindert** bin.	I have a wheelchair because I'm __________ .
ein großartiger Spieler mit viel **Talent**	a great player with lots of _______________
In welchem **Alter** darf man Auto fahren?	At what ____________ can you drive a car?
Im Alter von 18 verließ er die Schule.	He left school ____________________ 18.
Wie oft hat sie England **vertreten**?	How often did she _______________ England?
Er **interessiert sich** sehr **für** Kunst.	He'__ very ____________________ art.

14 Scrambled words: sport

Löse die Buchstabenrätsel, um Wörter zu finden, die mit Sport zusammenhängen.
Trage die deutschen Übersetzungen ein. Die markierten Buchstaben ergeben das „geheime Wort".

1 Foal Blot	F O O T B A L L	Fußball
2 Mal Ed	_ _ _ _ _	______________
3 Chain Mop	_ _ _ _ _ _ _ _	______________
4 Hem Tel	_ _ _ _ _ _	______________
5 Play Ten	_ _ _ _ _ _ _	______________
6 Glare Pekoe	_ _ _ _ _ _ _ _ _ _	______________
7 Dec Feen	_ _ _ _ _ _ _	______________

15 Word search

Finde Wörter im Rätsel, um die Wortgruppen zu vervollständigen. (↓ →)

G	H	D	S	A	U	S	A	G	E	L	O	C	B	K	R	H	B
O	A	A	P	E	V	O	L	L	E	Y	B	A	L	L	R	E	E
A	M	K	C	S	C	O	U	R	T	J	S	S	O	E	X	L	D
L	B	S	H	A	P	L	A	N	E	F	T	T	U	S	T	I	A
B	U	K	A	L	S	T	A	D	I	U	M	E	S	H	R	C	D
O	R	I	M	A	J	W	G	S	O	C	K	W	E	E	A	O	T
T	G	R	P	D	Z	B	L	S	G	S	K	I	S	L	M	P	I
R	E	T	I	U	W	Y	B	U	S	J	A	X	F	F	Y	T	G
O	R	S	O	F	U	N	D	E	R	G	R	O	U	N	D	E	H
U	F	O	N	T	M	C	Z	C	S	M	S	G	R	A	U	R	T
S	S	U	S	T	E	M	X	H	O	W	Q	P	N	T	W	P	S
E	H	P	H	A	D	S	R	I	F	K	X	C	I	H	A	G	V
R	O	Q	I	D	A	H	W	P	A	F	T	H	T	L	R	Z	F
S	R	X	P	J	L	O	M	S	S	G	A	A	U	E	D	T	E
J	T	S	D	S	X	E	M	C	H	N	B	I	R	T	R	A	R
Y	S	P	A	G	H	E	T	T	I	B	L	R	E	I	O	X	R
Q	P	I	Z	Z	A	K	U	I	P	U	E	G	O	C	B	I	Y
C	U	P	B	O	A	R	D	A	N	O	R	A	K	S	E	N	E

transport

bus

sport

athletics

room

clothes

food

17 Odd word out

Ein Wort passt nicht. Finde und unterstreiche es.

1 helmet – half-pipe – pads – swimsuit

2 stadium – referee – sports hall – court

3 stew – leotard – tights – shirt

4 church – castle – competition – community hall

5 player – medal – referee – coach

6 cup – defence – medal – prize

7 hairdresser – head teacher – engineer – celebrity

8 bridge – industry – road – tunnel

18 Crossword

Across

1 Badehose (8, 6)
5 Laufbahn (7, 5)
7 Spiel (5)
8 Sieg (3)
10 Tor (4)
14 Reitweg (6, 4)
17 Trainer/in (7)
18 Helm (6)
19 Endspiel (5)
21 Anhänger/in, Fan (9)

Down

1 Schwimmbecken (8, 4)
2 Laufschuhe (7, 5)
3 Stadion (7)
4 Skipiste (3, 5)
6 Mannschaft (4)
9 Halbzeit (4)
11 Sporthalle (5, 4)
12 Sattel (6)
13 Torwart, Torfrau (10)
15 trainieren (5)
16 Spielfeld (5)
20 Pokal (3)

New words ▸ pp. 72 – 73

Berlin hat 3,5 Millionen **Einwohner**.	The ______________ of Berlin is 3.5 million.
ein 25 **Quadratmeter** großes Wohnzimmer	a 25 ______________________ living room
Die Engländer sind eine **Nation** von Teetrinkern.	The English are a ____________ of tea drinkers.
Jagt eure Katze auch Mäuse?	Does your cat ____________ mice too?
Ist diese Musik **traditionell** oder modern?	Is this music _______________ or modern?
die **Lebensart** Südeuropas genießen	enjoy the _____________ in southern Europe
Du brauchst einen Schlafanzug für die **Schlafparty**.	You need pyjamas for the ______________ .
Am Wochenende gehen wir **richtig spät** ins Bett.	We go to bed _______________ at weekends.

1 Word groups

Trage die Wörter aus der Wolke in die richtigen Sterne ein.

actor – arrivals – choir – cleaner – cloudy – concert – farmer – fog – instrument – hairdresser
musician – painter – passengers – platforms – railway – rain – shop assistant – snow – song
stormy – sunny – ticket machines – toilets – trains – tune – 20 degrees

2 School words

Ergänze die fehlenden Wörter. Finde das „geheime Wort“ und übersetze es.

1 b o a r d — Jack, can you write the answers on the ★ please?

2 _ _ _ _ _ — We have lots of good singers in our school ★.

3 _ _ _ _ _ — I'm in the seventh ★ this year.

4 _ _ _ _ _ _ _ _ — How many ★ are there at your school? – About 800.

5 _ _ _ _ _ _ _ — In ★ you learn about the past.

6 _ _ _ _ _ _ _ — And in ★ you learn about flowers, animals, etc.

7 _ _ _ _ _ _ — I need a ★, not a pen.

8 _ _ _ _ _ _ _ — We have the same ★ for PE and English: Mr Hill.

9 _ _ _ — In ★ you learn how to draw and paint.

10 _ _ _ _ _ — In English we have to write an ★ about our hobbies.

The secret word is: Englisch ______________ *Deutsch* ______________

3 Lost words

Ergänze die Sätze mit den Wörtern im Feuerwerk.

1 I was really surprised at the size of the Canadian forests.

2 Moles are wild animals that live __________ the ground.

3 Jack is in hospital for an operation __________ his knee.

4 If you wait __________ Sue arrives, you'll be able to say hello.

5 I love being __________ the clouds when I travel by plane.

6 We live in the city centre, close __________ the big shops.

7 Mike was very upset __________ the bad news.

8 Anna moved her English books __________ a higher shelf.

9 There was no bridge at the river, so I couldn't get __________ .

10 Last night I dreamed __________ a holiday in Canada.

11 Kim listened __________ the key in the door, but nobody came.

12 I didn't like the party at first, but __________ the end it was OK.

New words ▸ p. 74

Erwachsene müssen mehr als Kinder zahlen.	____________ have to pay more than children.
Das Radio ist zu laut – **stell** es bitte **leiser**!	The radio's too loud – please _____ it _____ !
Geld liegt nicht auf der Straße.	______________________________ .
Schicke Jugendliche tragen oft die **neueste** Mode.	Trendy teens often wear the __________ fashion.
deine Familie **wichtig nehmen**	______________________ your family
Ich habe es nicht gekauft, weil es zu viel **kostete.**	I didn't buy it because it __________ too much.
Ich wollte nicht viel machen, nur **rumhängen.**	I didn't want to do much, just ____________ .
Gib das Geld vorsichtig aus! **Verschwende** es nicht!	Spend the money carefully! Don't __________ it!
Arbeit als Freiwilliger machen	do ______________________________

4 Word families

Finde die passenden Nomen zu den angegebenen Adjektiven.

1 crowded – crowd

2 dangerous – ______________

3 different – ______________

4 electric – ______________

5 noisy – ______________

6 spicy – ______________

7 active – ______________

8 beautiful – ______________

9 cloudy – ______________

10 industrial – ______________

5 Last letter – first letter

Der letzte Buchstabe von jedem Wort ist gleichzeitig der erste des nächsten Wortes.

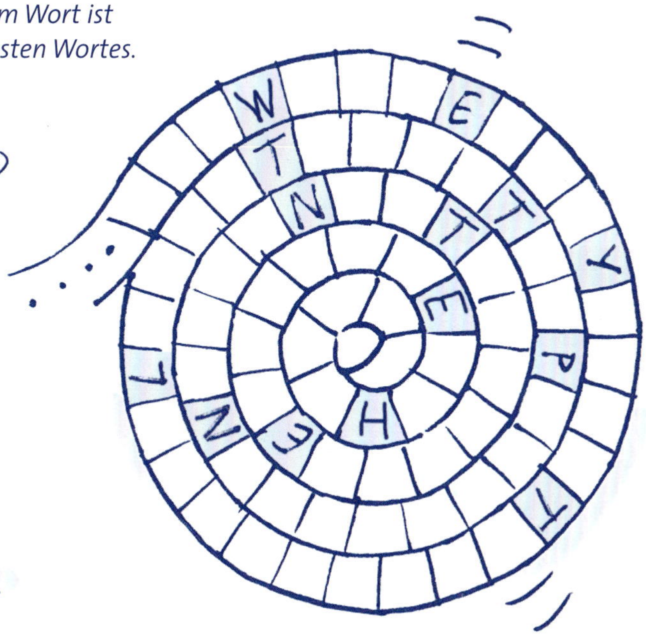

1 wachsen
2 verschwenden
3 Einsendung
4 Jogurt
5 traditionell
6 neuste(r, s)
7 Begabung
8 Falle
9 Einwohnerzahl
10 Nation
11 toll, fantastisch
12 übersetzen
13 umtauschen
14 jede(r, s)
15 Helm

6 Vocabulary network

Vervollständige das Wörternetz. Die Verben, die auf den Zetteln fehlen, bringt der Geier. Die anderen Wörter findest du im Sand.

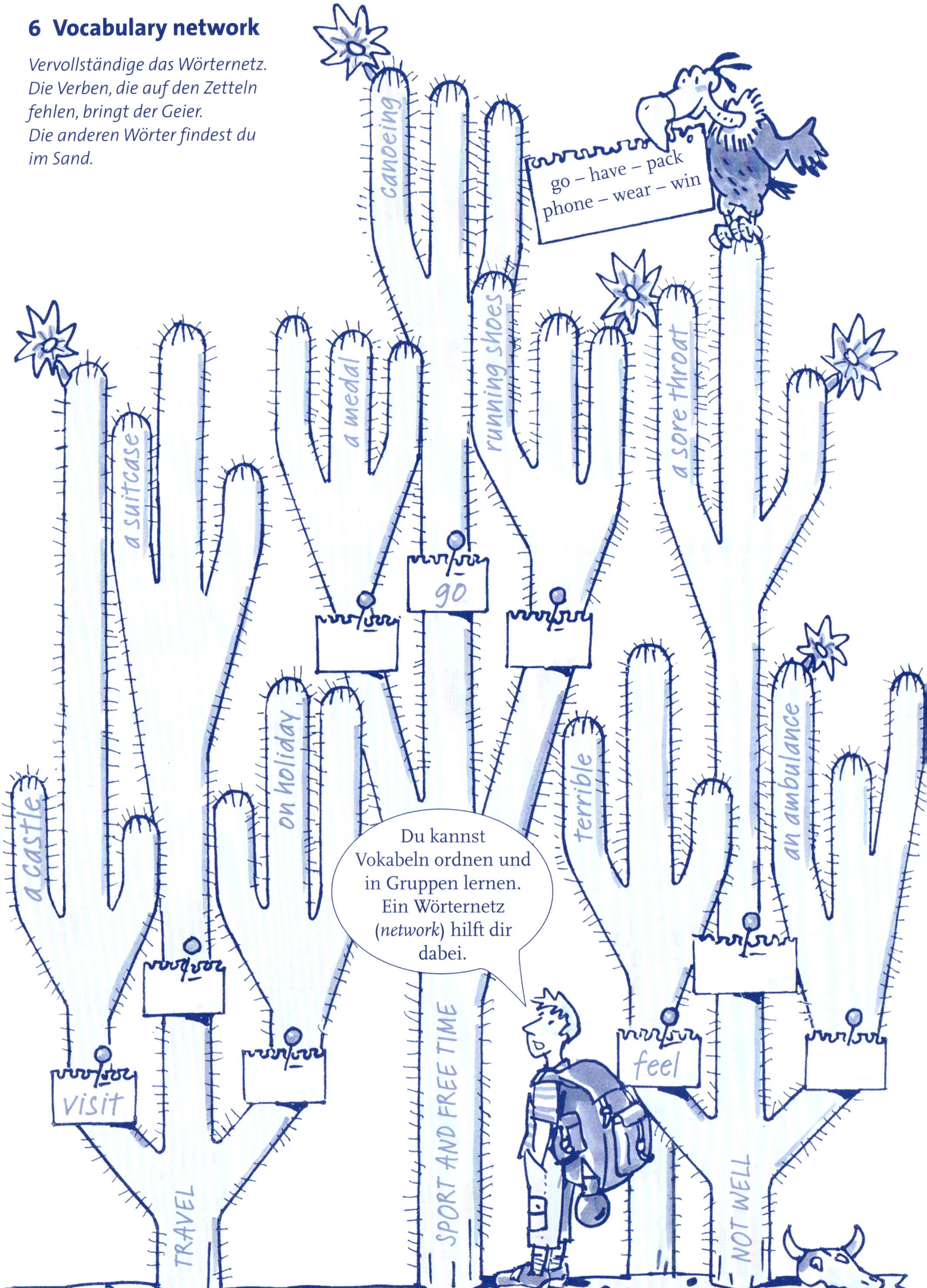

a bag – a cold – a cup – a doctor – a helmet – a museum – an old church – a rucksack – a prize
a temperature – by train – fishing – ill – on a boat trip – pads – snowshoeing – the hospital – weak

New words ▸ *p. 75*

Unsere Kinder besuchen eine Schule **am Ort**.	Our children go to a ________ school.
einkaufen im **Einkaufszentrum**	go shopping at the ________
Jeder hat die Chance zu gewinnen.	________ has the chance to win.
auf eine Frage **antworten**	________ a question
Die Musik ist OK, aber ich hasse den **Liedtext**.	The music is OK, but I hate the ________ .
Wir wollen spielen. Willst du **mitmachen**?	We want to play. Do you want to ________ ?
Sie war traurig und fing an zu **weinen**.	She was sad and started to ________ .
Kannst du wirklich seine Stimme **nachmachen**?	Can you really ________ his voice?
Unsere Eltern sind **streng**, aber fair.	Our parents are ________ but fair.
So ein Mist!	________ !
Ich weiß es nicht. Frag jemanden **anderes**.	I don't know. Ask somebody ________ .
eine Geschichte über einen **Drachen** lesen	read a story about a ________
Wo kann ich lernen, mit einem Kanu zu **paddeln**?	Where can I learn to ________ a canoe?
Das **Paddel** liegt neben dem Kanu.	The ________ is beside the canoe.

7 Word pairs

Welche Wörter passen zusammen?

New words ▸ pp. 76 – 77

Wir wohnen **in** der London Road.	We live ________ London Road.
Sue liebt Dan, aber Dan will mit Kim **ausgehen.**	Sue loves Dan, but Dan wants to ________ Kim.
Komm **gleich** nach der Schule nach Hause.	Come home ________________ after school.
ein Nachtklub mit einer riesigen **Tanzfläche**	a night club with a huge ________________
Im Gegensatz zu Deutschland ist Irland eine Insel.	________ Germany, Ireland is an island.
ein Boot in den Hafen **steuern**	________ a boat into the harbour
Habe ich es wirklich **richtig gemacht**?	Did I really ________ it ____________ ?
zum **Rhythmus** der Musik tanzen	dance to the ____________ of the music
Wir wohnten in einer **Hütte** in den Bergen.	We stayed in a ____________ in the mountains.
Das kann doch nicht dein Ernst sein!	________________ !
Er spielt den **selbstsicheren** Kerl in diesem Film.	He plays the ________________ guy in this movie.
Mensch, das ist ja großartig.	________ ! That's great!

8 Words with different meanings

Finde in der Liste die passenden Wörter zu den Paaren 1 – 7. Trage sie ein und unterstreiche die deutschen Entsprechungen.

1
a) auf der Nordseite des Platzes
b) 20 Quadratmeter
square

2
a) Fielen Tore in der ersten Halbzeit?
b) Möchtest du die Hälfte des Apfels?
____

3
a) Der Zug fährt um 17.30 ab.
b) Wir trainieren dreimal die Woche.
____

4
a) Was für ein Datum haben wir heute?
b) Willst du wirklich mit Alex ausgehen?
____

5
a) 120 Menschen passen in den Saal.
b) Du kannst deine Jacke im Flur aufhängen.
____

6
a) das Endspiel
b) die letzte Minute
____

7
a) einen Pokal gewinnen
b) Die Tasse ist schon in der Geschirrspülmaschine.
____

- cup
- date
- final
- half
- hall
- ~~square~~
- train

9 Word search

Im Rätsel sind 30 Tiere versteckt.
Finde und schreibe sie auf. (↓ →)

R	A	B	B	I	T	H	Y	C	H	U	I	B	G	B
L	N	R	O	N	P	E	W	H	O	C	C	T	I	U
T	W	F	G	P	N	D	H	I	R	D	R	B	R	D
I	U	R	S	A	M	G	A	C	S	Y	O	I	A	G
G	S	W	A	R	O	E	M	K	E	X	C	R	F	I
E	N	F	L	R	L	H	S	E	L	C	O	D	F	E
R	A	R	M	O	E	O	T	N	E	A	D	Y	E	S
K	K	O	O	T	P	G	E	U	P	T	I	X	F	Q
Q	E	G	N	P	C	I	R	S	H	Q	L	C	O	U
R	K	A	N	G	A	R	O	O	A	I	E	O	X	I
H	B	W	N	Z	F	L	I	O	N	Q	S	W	Y	R
I	E	S	W	D	O	G	U	S	T	A	H	J	U	R
N	A	K	W	O	O	D	P	E	C	K	E	R	S	E
O	R	F	S	M	O	U	S	E	R	A	E	L	U	L
M	O	N	K	E	Y	G	O	W	H	I	P	P	O	W

rabbit ____________ ____________

____________ ____________

10 Pronunciation

In jeder Wortgruppe gibt es bei zwei Wörtern stumme Buchstaben. Finde die Wörter und streiche die stummen Buchstaben durch.

Falls du nicht sicher bist, hilft die Lautschrift im Dictionary: z. B. **knife** [naɪf].

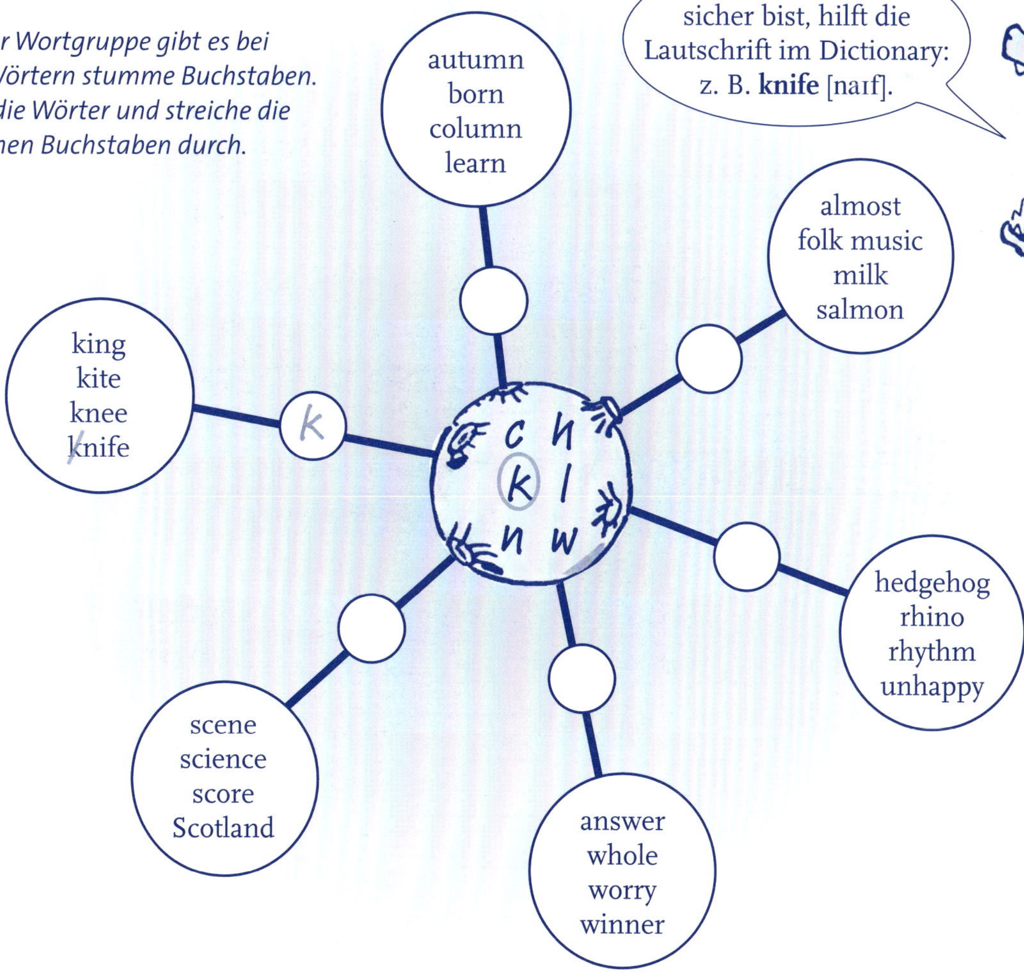

New words ▸ pp. 80 – 85

sich an die **Geschwindigkeitsbeschränkung** halten	keep to the ______________
Der Verkäufer **wog** die Zwiebeln.	The shop assistant ______________ the onions.
Über 10 **Prozent** der Briten leben in London.	Over 10 __________ of the British live in London.
Die Zimmer kosten 50 Euro **pro** Nacht.	The rooms cost 50 euros _____ night.
ein 30 **Kilogramm** schwerer Hund	a 30-______________ dog
Wie viele **Fischer** waren auf dem Boot?	How many ______________ were on the boat?
Sue **heiratete** einen Mann aus Deutschland.	Sue ______________ a man from Germany.
Übung vor dem Schreiben	______________
Bitte **brainstormt** so viele Ideen wie möglich.	Please ______________ as many ideas as possible.
Er braucht Geld, **damit** er ein Fahrrad kaufen kann.	He needs money __________ he can buy a bike.
mein Englisch in einem Sprachkurs **verbessern**	______________ my English in a language course
Er schreibt tolle Bücher – ich liebe seinen **Stil**.	He writes great books – I love his __________ .
Es ist **verrückt**, im Winter nur ein T-Shirt zu tragen.	It's __________ to wear just a T-shirt in winter.
Sie ist klug, aber sie hat oft **seltsame** Ideen.	She's clever, but she often has __________ ideas.
Das Zimmer ist 4 Meter lang und 3 Meter breit.	The room is 4 metres long and 3 metres _____ .
Angst vor dem Fliegen	______________ of flying
Schüttle deinen Kopf, um nein zu sagen.	______________ to say no.
Nicke, um ja zu sagen.	__________ to say yes.

11 One or two letters?

Trage die fehlenden Buchstaben ein: **d** *oder* **dd**, **f** *oder* **ff**, **n** *oder* **nn**

g/gg	a__g__ree, be____in, lan____uage, bi____est, fo____, fo____y
l/ll	ce____phone, adu____t, unti____, ta____ent, mode____, pu____over
m/mm	co____unity, swi____er, wo____an, gra____ar, mo____ent, thermo____eter
p/pp	po____ulation, sho____ing, pe____er, su____orter, re____resent, disa____ear
r/rr	tomo____ow, ma____ied, guita____, ti____ed, hu____y, di____ections
s/ss	ba____ket, e____ay, gla____es, gue____, hu____band, i____land
t/tt	bo____le, wa____er, pre____y, wea____her, spaghe____i

12 More about ... traditional Inuit hunting

Vervollständige den Text mit Wörtern aus der Box.

The Inuit live in Greenland and in the north of Canada, where winter temperatures (1) can be minus 40 degrees Celsius. So it's ___________ (2) too cold to have farm animals or to *grow food. That's why hunting and ___________ (3) were once a big part of Inuit life. The meat of sea animals like the *walrus or the whale, or of ___________ (4) animals like the polar bear, was traditional Inuit food. And of course, hunting wasn't ___________ (5) important for food. The Inuit could also use animal *skins to make clothes. In the past, when the Inuit hunted sea animals they used a *kayak*, a ___________ (6) of canoe. And on land they ___________ (7) sledges with dogs. A team of dogs could easily pull 20 kilos. And dogs ___________ (8) smell very well too, so they could help the Inuit to find the animals. Sometimes a hunting trip took a few days, so the Inuit often ___________ (9) little igloos when they needed a place to sleep at night. Inside an igloo, the temperature could be ___________ (10) 20 degrees Celsius when it was only minus 40 outside.

grow = anbauen; walrus = Walross; skin = Fell

built could fishing used
land much kind plus
just ~~temperatures~~

13 Odd word out

Finde und unterstreiche das Wort, das nicht passt.

1 kilometre – minute – metre – centimetre
2 lyrics – painting – photo – picture
3 seven – per cent – eight – nine
4 cellphone – text message – mobile – telephone
5 eyes – build – glasses – see
6 crazy – mad – ready – weird
7 shout – speak – whisper – weigh
8 large – local – medium – small
9 adults – children – teenagers – engineers
10 mall – café – supermarket – department store
11 journey – ride – trip – map
12 cow – dragon – horse – sheep

New words ▸ *pp. 88 – 89*

zwei Nächte auf einem **Zeltplatz** verbringen	spend two nights at a ___________
Es ist billiger zu **zelten**, als im Hotel zu wohnen.	It's cheaper to ___________ than to stay at a hotel.
Wieviele **Aufseher** kümmern sich um den Park?	How many ___________ look after the park?
Diese **Stromschnellen** sind für Boote gefährlich.	These ___________ are dangerous for boats.
Kanus sind kleine und schnelle Boote.	___________ are small, fast boats.
Auf diesem Fluss habe ich gelernt, **Kanu** zu **fahren**.	I learned to ___________ on this river.
Warum **greifen** Bären Menschen **an**?	Why do bears ___________ people?
Aktivitäten **im Freien** machen im Sommer Spaß.	___________ activities are fun in summer.
englische Alltags**ausdrücke** lernen	learn English everyday ___________

14 The fourth word

Welches Wort fehlt hier?

1 one – thousand / metre – ___________

2 murder – murderer / photograph – ___________

3 he – they / his – ___________

4 green – colour / two – ___________

5 parrot – bird /piano – ___________

6 days – month / months – ___________

7 day – sun / night – ___________

8 man – men / knife – ___________

9 yes – no / nod – ___________ (your head)

10 laugh – happy / cry – ___________

15 Spot the mistakes

In jedem Satz sind zwei Fehler. Unterstreiche und korrigiere sie.

1 When childs are young they often has teddy bears. children ___________

2 Bears can look realy sweet and lots off people love them. ___________ ___________

3 But they are allso large and very danger animals. ___________ ___________

4 They usualy hunt at night or in the errly morning. ___________ ___________

5 Bears can ran quickly and they are great swimers. ___________ ___________

6 It's very interresting to watch how a bear catches salmons. ___________ ___________

7 It stand in the river and waits quitely for a long time. ___________ ___________

8 When the bare sees a fish it jump and catches it. ___________ ___________

15 Opposites

Trage die Gegenteile der fettgedruckten Wörter in die Lücken ein.

1 have **friendly** / ______________ neighbours

2 Do you really **agree** / ____________ with me?

3 wears **old-fashioned** / __________ clothes

4 turn the music **down** / __________

5 **plus** / __________ 10 degrees Celsius

6 a **strong** / __________ swimmer

7 at the **top** / __________ of the shelf

8 **forget** / ______________ an important date

9 a **sad** / __________ ending

10 find a **husband** / ______________

11 an **exciting** / a ______________ film

12 a really **hot** / ____________ day

13 a **clean** / ____________ city

14 Wait **downstairs** / __________ in your room!

17 Number crossword

Gleiche Zahlen sind gleiche Buchstaben. Die angegebenen Lösungen helfen dir, das gesamte Rätsel zu lösen.

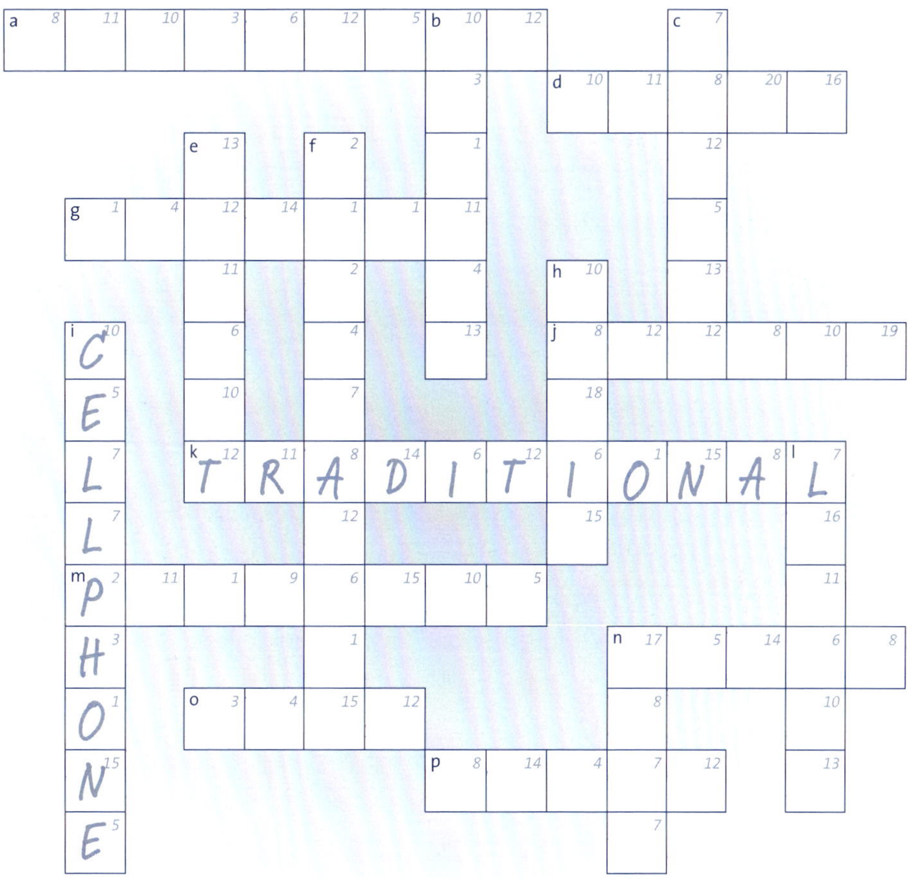

Wo im Rätsel findet man das englische Wort für ...

Provinz	m across	Angriff	__________	streng	__________
Hütte	h down	Erwachsene(r)	__________	Einwohnerzahl	__________
Jagd	__________	verrückt	__________	Einkaufszentrum	__________

Unit 5

New words ▸ pp. 94–95

Dies musst du selbst entscheiden.	______________________
Was habt ihr **bis jetzt** in den Ferien gemacht?	What have you done ________ in the holidays?
Bitte lest **die folgenden** drei Zeilen.	Please read ______________________ three lines.
Diese Zeitung hat einen tollen Sport**teil**.	This paper has a great sport ________________ .
Ein **Redakteur** überprüft und korrigiert Texte.	An _____________ checks and corrects texts.
Willst du den Artikel **veröffentlichen**?	Do you want to ______-___________ the article?
Was ist besser: ein Foto oder eine **Zeichnung**?	What's better: a photo or a ________________ ?
Zeichne ein Bild deines Traumhauses!	_____________ a picture of your dream house!
Setze dich mit ihm über das Telefon **in Verbindung.**	____________________ him by phone.
Unser Wohltätigkeitsbasar war wieder ein **Erfolg**.	Our jumble sale was a ________________ again.
Ich trage **Kopfhörer**, wenn ich Musik spiele.	I wear ________________ when I play music.
in ein **Mikrofon** sprechen	speak into a ___________________________
Wie groß ist dein Computer**bildschirm**?	How big is your computer ________________ ?

1 Pronunciation

Ordne die Wörter aus der Box der richtigen Aussprachegruppe zu.

ʊ	juː	ʌ

~~bully~~ bus ~~computer~~ community excuse full ~~fun~~ huge menu publish pull put push sugar summer tunnel tube trumpet

ʊ	juː	ʌ
bully	*computer*	*fun*

2 The fourth word

Welches Wort wird hier gesucht?

1 banana – fruit / potato – ____________

2 lunch – meal / Chicken Tikka – ____________

3 salmon – fish / woodpecker – ____________

4 castle – building / armchair – ____________

5 skis – sports equipment / pullover – ____________

6 dishwasher – machine / piano – ____________

7 Britain – island / Uranus – ____________

8 seven – number / pink – ____________

9 song – music / painting – ____________

10 mole – wild animal / cow – ____________ animal

3 Making phrases

Vervollständige die Audrücke mit einem Verb aus der Box.

1 fall ____________ down the stairs

2 ____________ down the radio a bit

3 ____________ out in the evening with friends

4 ____________ what you read in the newspaper

5 ____________ with my partner's ideas

6 ____________ up in a big city

7 ____________ up a word I don't know

8 ____________ somebody around the town

4 Opposites

Trage die Gegenteile der fett gedruckten Wörter in die Lücken ein.

1 the **best** / ____________ book I've ever read

2 be **good** / ____________ at French

3 at the **bottom** / ____________ of the street

4 **bright** / ____________ colours

5 a **healthy** / an ____________ meal

6 be **sure** / ____________ about the answer

7 arrive **early** / ____________ for the lesson

8 a **tidy** / an ____________ room

9 **in front of** / ________________ the house

10 a good **answer** / ____________

11 live **above** / ____________ ground

12 a **fair** / an ____________ question

13 look **left** / ____________

14 **remember** / ____________ to phone a friend

New words ▸ p. 96

Überfliegt den Text, aber lest ihn nicht im Detail. — ______ the text, but don't read it in detail.

Wir fanden keine Antwort auf das **Rätsel**. — We didn't find an answer to the ______ .

Ist deine Jacke **aus Leder gemacht**? — Is your jacket ______ ?

Sherlock Holmes rauchte **Pfeife**. — Sherlock Holmes smoked a ______ .

Eine Flasche **ragte aus** der Einkaufstasche **heraus**. — A bottle ______ of the shopping bag.

Ein kalter Wind **wehte** aus dem Westen. — A cold wind ______ from the west.

Fleisch muss man im Kühlschrank **aufbewahren**. — You have to ______ meat in the fridge.

Er **drückte** ihre Hand und lächelte. — He ______ her hand and smiled.

Bitte spiele nur die ersten beiden **Töne**. — Please play only the first two ______ .

5 Word families

Finde die passenden Verben zu den angegebenen Nomen.

1 announcement – announce
2 comparison – ______
3 explanation – ______
4 drawing – ______
5 ending – ______
6 life – ______
7 attack – ______
8 supporter – ______
9 laughter – ______
10 meaning – ______

6 The best word

Finde das Wort in der Strickleiter, das am besten in die Lücke passt.

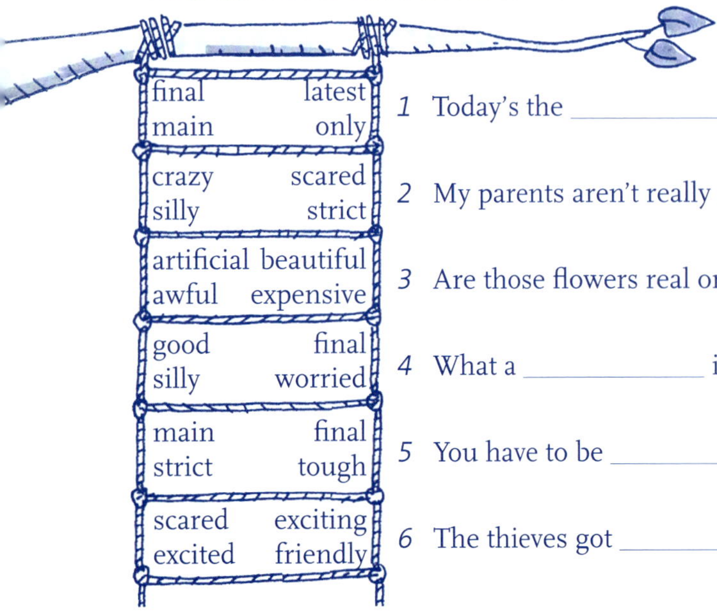

1 Today's the ______ day of the holidays. Tomorrow we go back to school.
2 My parents aren't really ______ – they let me do most things I want.
3 Are those flowers real or ______ ?
4 What a ______ idea! It will never work!
5 You have to be ______ to survive in wild country.
6 The thieves got ______ and ran away.

New words ▸ *pp. 97 – 98*

Der Zweite Welt**krieg** begann 1939.	World ________ II started in 1939.
Martin muss für den Englischtest **lernen**.	Martin has to ________ for the English test.
Wir können in ein Konzert oder in die **Oper** gehen.	We can go to a concert or to the ________ .
Papa studierte an einer **Hochschule** im Ausland.	Dad studied at a ________ abroad.
Wir **machen** dich zu einem Tennisstar!	We'll ________ you a tennis star!
Wird die Band eine neue CD **herausbringen**?	Is the band going to ________ a new CD?
Es tut mir leid, aber die Karten sind **ausverkauft**.	I'm sorry, but the tickets are ________ .
Wie viele **Titel** gibts auf der CD?	How many ________ are there on the CD?
Wie lang sind die Sommer**ferien** in Kanada?	How long is summer ________ in Canada?
Ein schöner Strand ist ein **Paradies** für mich.	A beautiful beach is ________ for me.
Ich mag ein **weiches** Bett lieber als ein hartes.	I like a ________ bed better than a hard one.
eine neue **Stereoanlage** kaufen	buy a new ________
Monopoly ist eines der **klassischen** Spiele.	Monoply is one of ________ games.
Nun **Leute**, was wollen wir heute machen?	Well ________ ,what are we going to do today?
Heute Nacht **werde ich** 500 km **gereist sein**.	Tonight ________ 500 km.
Sei bitte **spätestens bis** 10 Uhr zu Hause.	Please be at home ____ 10 o'clock.
Am Wochenende kann ich **ausspannen**.	I can ________ at the weekend.

7 Last letter – first letter

Der letzte Buchstabe von jedem Wort ist gleichzeitig der erste des nächsten Wortes.

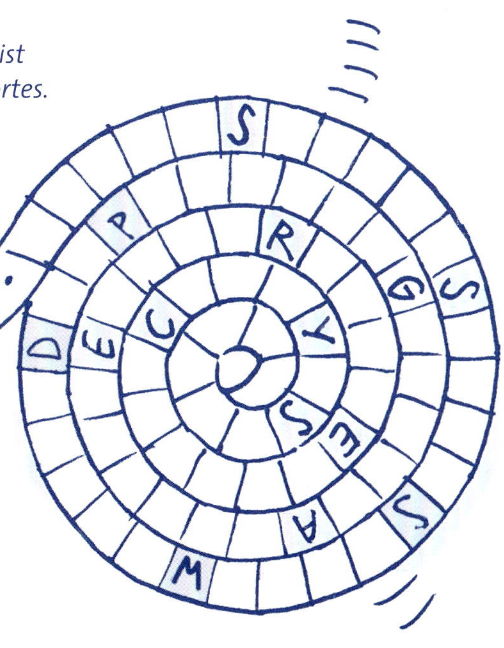

1 Helden
2 Erfolg
3 Sehenswürdigkeiten
4 Schatten
5 besorgt
6 fallen lassen
7 Gemälde
8 Oma
9 bekanntgeben
10 Redakteur
11 Scherzfrage
12 elektrisch
13 verrückt
14 ja
15 Abschnitt

New words ▸ p. 99

Wann bist du heute Morgen **aufgewacht**?	When did you ______________ this morning?
Bitte **weck** mich morgen um sieben Uhr.	Please ______________ me tomorrow at 7 o'clock.
Dieser **Radiosender** spielt tolle Musik.	This ______________ plays great music.
Warum **stürzt** mein Computer so oft **ab**?	Why does my computer ______________ so often?
Heb das Papier **auf** und wirf es in die Mülltonne!	______________ the paper ___ and throw it in the bin!
neue **Trommelstöcke** für unser Konzert kaufen	buy new ______________ for our concert
Zu meinem **Entsetzen** fing er an zu weinen.	To my ______________ he started to cry.
Leider ist sie auf einem Ohr **taub**.	I'm afraid she's ______________ in one ear.
Ich sagte nichts, weil **es keinen Sinn hatte**.	I said nothing because ______________ .
Ich las die **Schlagzeilen**, keine ganzen Berichte.	I read the ______________ , not whole reports.
Wir kennen **uns** – wir sind alte Freunde.	We know ______________ – we're old friends.

8 Word search - The media

15 englische Begriffe aus dem Wortfeld „Medien“ sind im Rätsel versteckt. Finde sie und übersetze sie ins Deutsche. (↓ →)

S	N	E	W	S	P	A	P	E	R	C	I
T	H	R	H	O	L	G	D	H	M	K	T
A	Y	E	E	R	I	N	G	T	O	N	E
T	C	P	A	R	E	C	O	R	D	M	L
I	E	O	D	M	A	G	A	Z	I	N	E
O	L	R	P	E	D	I	T	O	R	M	V
N	L	T	H	C	G	S	Q	G	U	E	I
N	P	R	O	G	R	A	M	M	E	H	S
B	H	N	N	A	R	T	I	C	L	E	I
C	O	X	E	L	B	N	E	W	S	O	O
M	N	G	S	P	U	B	L	I	S	H	N
E	E	X	Q	G	M	O	N	I	T	O	R

newspaper – Zeitung
____
____
____
____
____
____
____
____
____
____
____
____
____
____

9 Words in pictures: fruit and vegetables

a) Wie heißt das abgebildete Obst und Gemüse? Trage die Wörter in die nummerierten Lücken ein.

3

5

1

2

4

6

9

10
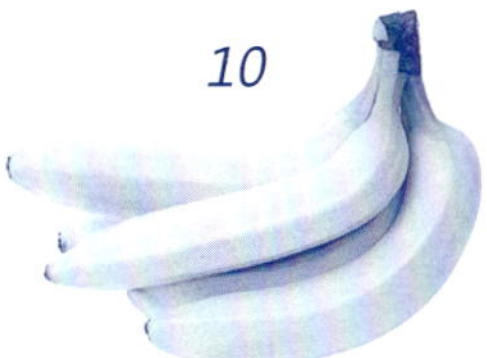

8

7

1 bright long red tomatoes

2 large windy round ______

3 sweet Spanish spicy ______

4 short hard green ______

5 big grey garden ______

6 delicious German neat ______

7 bright round orange ______

8 healthy green empty ______

9 delicious sunny new ______

10 long yellow German ______

b) 2 von 3 Adjektiven passen zu den Wörtern, die du eingetragen hast. Unterstreiche sie.

10 Word building

Verbinde ein Wort aus den Steinen mit einem Wort aus der Liste. Trage die deutsche Übersetzung ein.

Wenn man Nomen miteinander verbindet, schreibt man sie mal auseinander, mal zusammen.

Eine Regel gibt es leider nicht. Also merkt euch die Einzelfälle!

1 pop station Popsender

2 ______ floor ______

3 ______ room ______

4 ______ shoes ______

5 ______ message ______

6 half-time ______

7 ______ grandfather ______

8 classroom ______

9 ______ line ______

10 ______ chair ______

New words ▸ pp. 100–105

Lehrer dürfen Schüler nicht **schlagen**.	Teachers aren't allowed to __________ students.
Er ist sehr **beliebt** – jeder mag ihn.	He's very ______________ – everyone likes him.
Thomas Edison war ein berühmter **Erfinder**.	Thomas Edison was a famous ______________ .
Wie viele Menschen arbeiten für diese **Firma**?	How many people work for this ____________ ?
Könntest du bitte die Karte unterschreiben?	Could you ____________ sign the card, please?
ein kaputtes Fernsehgerät **reparieren**	________________ a broken TV
Eine Gitarre hat sechs **Saiten**.	A guitar has six ____________ .
Diese Schule hat sehr strenge **Regeln**.	This school has very strict __________ .
Trink keinen **Alkohol**, bevor du fährst.	Don't drink ______________ before you drive.
Ich muss laufen – die Busfahrer **streiken**.	I have to walk – the bus drivers are on __________ .
Es war dein Fehler – **gib** mir nicht **die Schuld**!	It was your mistake – don't ______________ me!
Die **Biografie** erzählt viel über sein Leben.	The ______________ tells us a lot about his life.
Fangen Nomen mit **Großbuchstaben** an?	Do nouns start with ________________________ ?
Ist dieses Verb **regelmäßig** oder **unregelmäßig**?	Is this verb ____________ or ______________ ?
Ist simple past hier die richtige **Zeit**?	Is simple past the right ____________ here?
ein **Karriere** in einer großen Firma	a ____________ in a big company
eine **Recherche** für einen Aufsatz über Musik	________________ for an essay on music
Muss ich hier **Anführungszeichen** benutzen?	Do I have to use ________________________ here?
eine **genaue** Beschreibung des Diebes geben	give an ______________ description of the thief

11 Verb forms

Ergänze die Tabelle der unregelmäßigen Verben.

1	do	did	done
2		blew	
3	cost		
4		drew	
5			fought
6	grow		

7	hang out		
8		hid	
9		kept	
10			shaken
11		slept	
12	wake		

12 Hidden words

*Ergänze die Wortgruppen, indem du Wörter mit Buchstaben der Wörter **„musical instruments"**¹ bildest.*

¹ *Musikinstrumente*

13 Definitions

Vervollständige die Definitionen mit Wörtern aus den Mauersteinen. Trage die richtigen Wörter aus Kens Zeitung in die rechte Spalte ein.

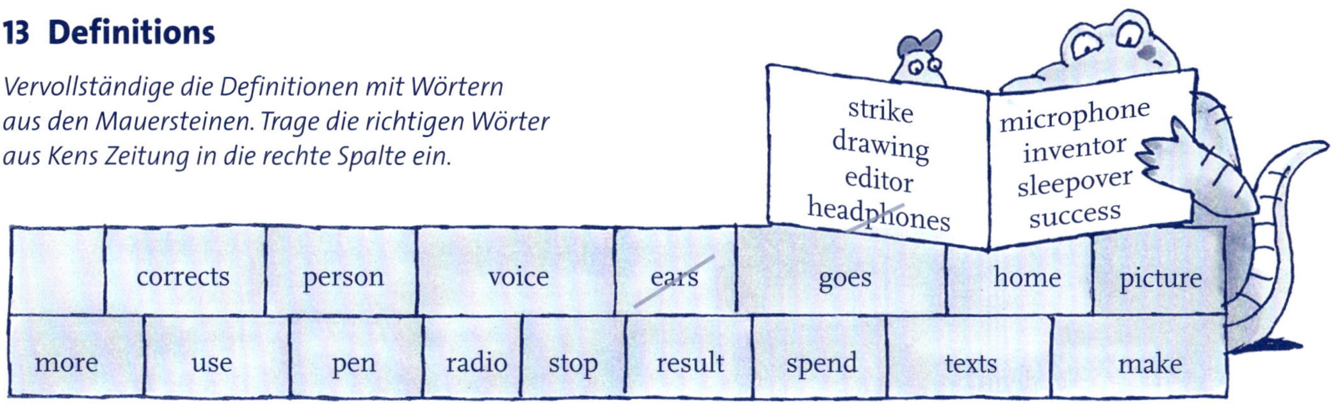

1 Wear these over your *ears* to listen to an mp3 player or the ________ . *headphones*

2 when people ________ work because they want ________ money ________

3 when you ________ the night at a friend's ________ ________

4 someone who checks and ________ articles and other ________ ________

5 the first ________ to think of something or ________ something ________

6 a ________ that you make with a pencil or ________ ________

7 when something ________ well and there's a good ________ ________

8 something that you ________ to make a ________ louder ________

14 What are the words?

Bilde Nomen mit –er oder –or.
Trage die deutsche Übersetzung ein.

1 actor – Schauspieler/in
2 collect____ – ____________
3 support____ – ____________
4 farm____ – ____________
5 visit____ – ____________
6 football____ – ____________
7 edit____ – ____________
8 report____ – ____________
9 explore____ – ____________
10 invent____ – ____________

15 Word friends

Welche Wörter auf den Steinen passen in die Lücken?

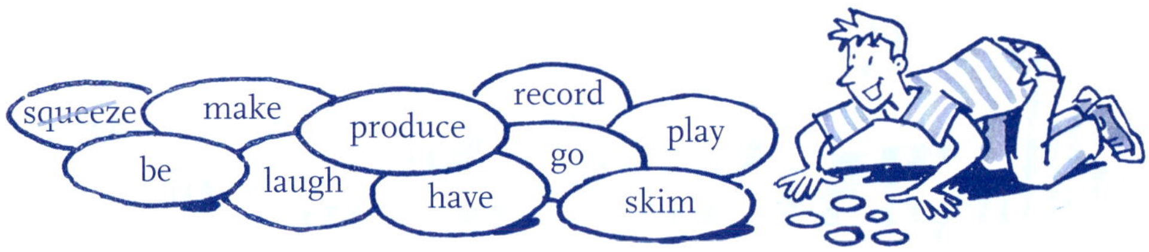

1 squeeze somebody's arm / an orange
2 ____________ a newspaper / cars / computers
3 ____________ a point / a phone call / a deal
4 ____________ a new CD / a single / a song
5 ____________ a trick on sb. / hockey / the drums
6 ____________ on strike / to school / well
7 ____________ good at sth. / surprised / sold out
8 ____________ a cold /a good time / an argument
9 ____________ at a joke / at another person / loudly
10 ____________ an article / the first page / the report

16 Scrambled words: American and British English

Die Buchstabenrätsel ergeben Wörter aus dem amerikanischen Englisch. Trage diese und ihre britischen Entsprechungen ein. Die Tipps helfen dir.

		American English	British English	Tip
1	omm	mom	mum	Not your dad!
2	necellhop			Contact people with this.
3	leetavor			Go up or down in this.
4	waybus			Railway below ground.
5	cavaniot			No school now.

17 Hour glasses

Übersetze die Wörter und trage sie in die passende Sanduhr ein.

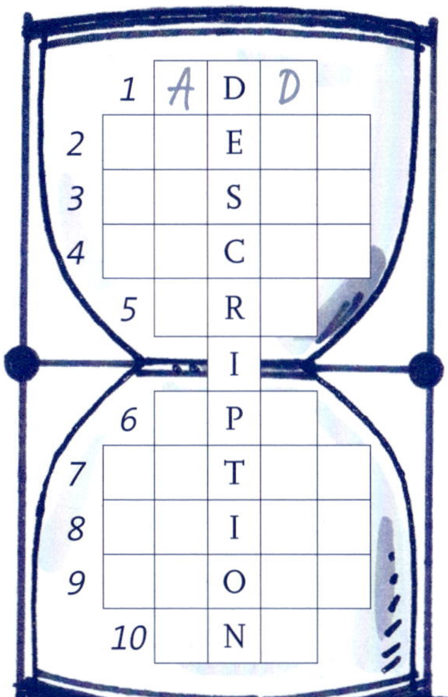

1 aß – hinzufügen
2 Königin – schmutzig
3 aufgebracht – Strand
4 Medaille – Tatsachen
5 versuchen – Kind
6 Mülltonne – Spion
7 Chor – bis
8 Endspiel – ruhig
9 Beweis – Bühne
10 Schluss – krank

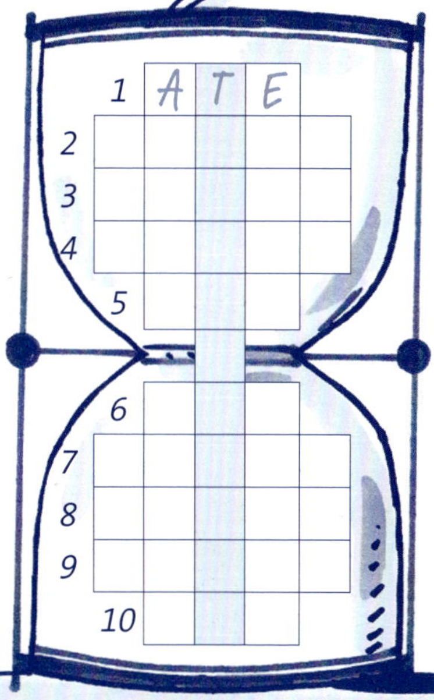

Das geheime Wort in der rechten Sanduhr heißt: Englisch ____________

Deutsch ____________

18 Word ladder

Gehe von unten nach oben, indem du bei jeder Sprosse einen Buchstaben veränderst.

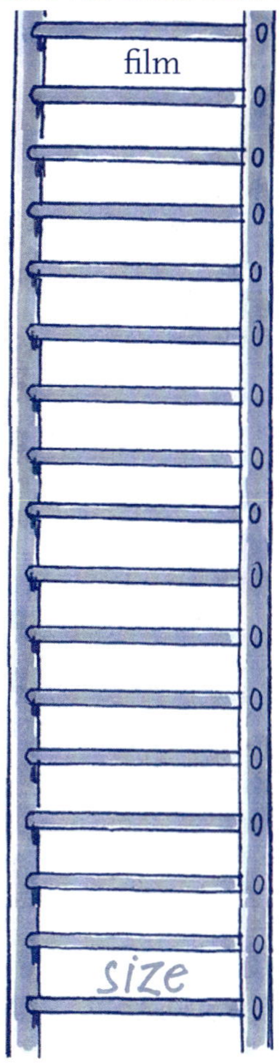

another word for movie
Click here to download the sound ★.
I was ill last week but I'm ★ again now.
Which underground ★ goes to St Paul's Cathedral?
This isn't my bag – ★ is blue, not black
Germany – kilometre, Britain and America – ★
a small black animal that lives under the ground
I lost some money because there was a ★ in my pocket.
Did you get a ★ in the school play?
Can you explain this grammar ★ please?
A ★ person is unfriendly to other people.
When did you learn to ★ a horse?
Let's ★ behind this wall. Then nobody will see us.
It's a long walk to the water when the ★ is out.
Which ★ of the street is number 47?
What ★ is this T-shirt? Medium or large?

19 Crossword

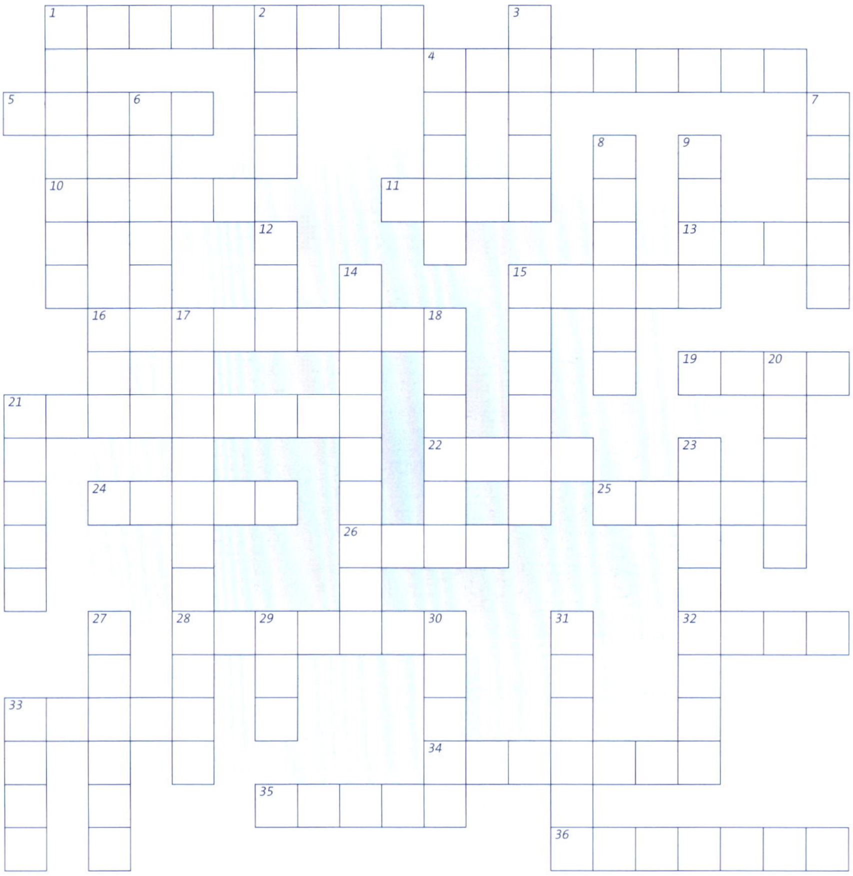

Across

1 American English for 'mobile phone' (9)
4 the story of a somebody's life (9)
5 You need it to cut bread. (5)
10 opposite of 'late' (5)
11 simple past of 'wake' (4)
13 a name for the underground in London (4)
15 Somebody stole my bike ★ I was in the shop. (5)
16 In this sport, you run, jump, etc. (9)
19 a big shopping centre (4)
21 cupboards, chairs, sofas, wardrobes, etc. (9)
22 60 minutes – an hour / 30 minutes – ★ an hour (4)
24 newspapers, magazines, radio, TV, the Internet, etc. (5)
25 a person who trains a sports team (5)
26 the person at work who tells you what you have to do (4)
28 Hard work is the key to ★ ! (10)
32 from all ★ England = from every part of England (4)
33 one – once / two – ★ (5)
34 the main city in a country (7)
35 not very clever; stupid (5)
36 a building where you can watch a football match (7)

Down

1 when people play music for an audience (7)
2 very, very big (4)
3 children – child / mice – ★ (5)
4 opposite of 'above' (5)
6 opposite of 'remember' (6)
7 The wife of a king is a ★ . (5)
8 I like films with a happy ★ . (6)
9 opposite of 'love' (4)
12 I'm 14. What ★ are you? (3)
14 This tells you when your lessons start and finish. (9)
15 They're round. A car has got four of them. (6)
16 We need it to live. (3)
17 a person who washes and cuts hair (11)
18 the things that tourists like to see (6)
20 Can you turn on the ★ ? It's so dark here. (5)
21 the game to find the winner, always the last game in a series (5)
23 October 3rd is a ★ holiday in Germany (8)
27 a person who checks and corrects texts (6)
29 A team that wins a final often gets this prize. (3)
30 opposite of 'mild' (5)
31 the words of a song (6)
33 make – made / take – ★ (4)

Bye, Ken!
Hellooo ... We're going to have fun together! In Wordmaster A4.
WM

Anhang: * Wörter

Introduction New words ▸ *pp. 7–11*

zu einem **Konzert** mit klassischer Musik gehen	go to a ____________ with classical music
Ich **nehme an**, dass du wieder Pizza essen willst!	I ____________ you want to eat pizza again!
Ich bin **hungrig** – ich habe noch nicht gegessen.	I'm ____________ – I haven't eaten yet.
Ich bin **durstig** – gib mir bitte etwas Wasser.	I'm ____________ – Give me some water, please.
Du bist **eine halbe Stunde** zu früh!	You're ____________ early!
Wunderbares Wetter! Warm, viel Sonne ...	____________ weather! Warm, lots of sun ...

Unit 1 Lost words ▸ *pp. 12–17*

Ergänze die Sätze mit fünf Wörtern aus dem Feuerwerk.

1 It was the first ________ that we stayed in Spain.

2 The flight from London was ________ – only £50!

3 We spent the ________ day outside in the sun.

4 One day we met some nice German ________ on the beach.

5 And we saw the king and the rest of the ________ family.

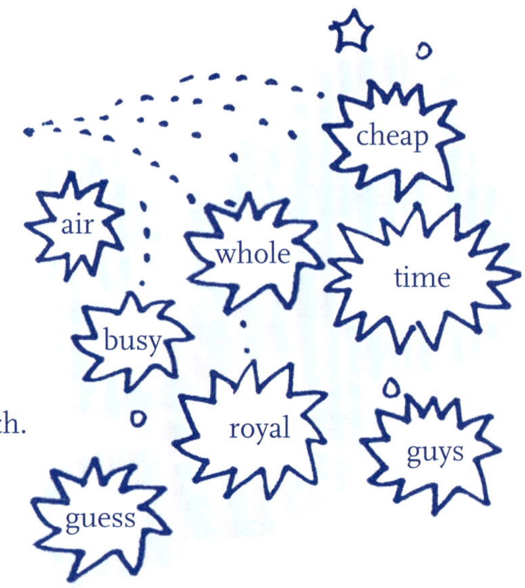

Unit 1 Scrambled words ▸ *pp. 18–28*

Löse die Buchstabenrätsel, um die fehlenden Wörter zu finden.

1	s o c a t	I really love the sea air here on the ________ .
2	o f l w r s e	You've got some really beautiful ________ in your garden.
3	c o i v e	Fantastic singer! Great ________ !
4	d e r i t i c n o s	I don't know the way. We'll have to ask somebody for ________ .
5	d e r g a n	Is it safe to go in here? – Yes, of course. I can't see any ________ .

Unit 2 New words ▸ p. 32–35

Mein Handy piepst – es ist eine **SMS**.	My mobile's bleeping – it's a ______________ .
Du kannst mich anrufen, oder **eine SMS schicken**.	You can phone me or __________ me.
Wie du weißt, kann es in Schottland kühl sein.	_______ you know, it can be cool in Scotland.
einen **Dokumentarfilm** über Wales ansehen	watch a ________________ about Wales
Ich **konnte** mit sechs schwimmen.	I was ____________ to swim when I was six.
sich für Pizza oder für Spaghetti **entscheiden**	________________ between pizza or spaghetti

Unit 2 Word pairs ▸ pp. 39–47

Welche Wörter passen zusammen?
*(Alle *Wörter aus Unit 2 sind gekennzeichnet.)*

Unit 3 New words ▸ pp. 56–69

Unsere Schule hat ein neues Hockey**feld**.	Our school has got a new hockey __________ .
Wer **präsentierte** gestern die Sport**nachrichten**?	Who ____________ the sports _______ yesterday?
Heute spielt Liverpool **gegen** den Meister.	Today Liverpool plays __________ the champions.
Dieser **Wald** hat sehr große Bäume.	These ____________ have got very tall trees.
Amerika wurde von Columbus **entdeckt**.	America was _______________ by Columbus.
Darf man in Museen Fotos machen?	Are you ____________ to take photos in museums?
Darf ich bitte das Fenster öffnen?	_______ I open the window please?

Units 4 and 5 New words ▸ pp. 7–11

Er kann nicht singen und **auch nicht** spielen.	He can't sing, and he ca_____ act __________ .
Es ist schade, dass ihr nicht kommen könnt.	__________ that you can't come.
Mein kleiner Hund folgt mir **überall** hin.	My little dog follows me __________ .
Sind Fußballspieler die **Helden** von heute?	Are footballers today's __________ ?
Oje! Ich habe meinen Zug gerade **verpasst**.	Oh dear. I've just __________ my train.
Was **produziert** diese Fabrik?	What does this factory __________ ?
Ausdrücke für einen Urlaub im Ausland lernen	learn __________ for a holiday abroad
einen **Artikel** für eine Zeitung schreiben	write an __________ for a newspaper
Dieses Sofa ist etwas weich, aber **bequem**.	This sofa is a bit soft, but __________ .
Er war so traurig – er hatte **Tränen** in den Augen.	He was so sad – he had __________ in his eyes .
Mit dieser **Maschine** kannst du Brot machen.	You can make bread with this __________ .
Wo kann ich meinen Namen in die Liste **eintragen**?	Where can I __________ my name on the list?

Units 4 and 5 Odd word out

Finde und unterstreiche das Wort, das nicht passt.

1 piano – clarinet – machine – trumpet
2 hero – engineer – doctor – teacher
3 phrase – sentence – paragraph – editor
4 small – comfortable – medium – large
5 paramedic – photographer – performer – produce
6 also – either – article – too
7 eye – ear– tear – nose
8 here – there – everywhere – tomorrow
9 many – miss – much – most
10 pity – pretty – nice – beautiful

Units 4 and 5 Spot the mistakes

In jedem Satz sind zwei Fehler. Unterstreiche und korrigiere sie.

1 I mist my train, so I won't be able to visit you these weekend. missed __________
2 There was snow everywere, so we arriving late at the station. __________ __________
3 It's a real pitty – I real wanted to see you again. __________ __________
4 I haven't see you for weeks, and I haven't seen your mum ither. __________ __________
5 Please tell her I liked the artikel she sent me about football heros. __________ __________

Introduction

1 Crossword

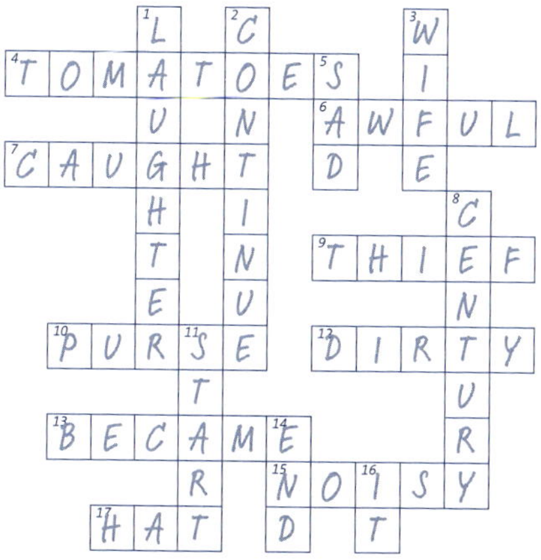

2 Verb forms

2 show – showed – shown
3 spend – spent – spent
4 hide – hid – hidden
5 do – did – done
6 take – took – taken
7 fly – flew – flown
8 read – read – read
9 throw – threw – thrown
10 speak – spoke – spoken
11 write – wrote – written
12 ride – rode – ridden

3 Lost words

1 In, 2 of, 3 from, 4 to,
5 at, 6 by, 7 for

4 Last letter – first letter

1 drum 2 mixture 3 electric
4 concert 5 trumpet 6 trombone
7 enough 8 half 9 fiddle
10 elevator 11 recorder

5 Word search

W	Y	H	D	T	K	X	Z	L	N
M	Y	Q	R	T	K	K	W	M	R
J	O	O	U	F	I	D	D	L	E
T	R	O	M	B	O	N	E	F	C
P	T	R	U	M	P	E	T	L	O
I	C	G	N	H	F	B	D	U	R
A	Z	C	E	L	L	O	M	T	D
N	V	N	U	U	H	P	Z	E	E
O	G	U	I	T	A	R	B	K	R
S	A	X	O	P	H	O	N	E	Y

piano – Klavier
cello – Cello
drum – Trommel
flute – Querflöte
recorder – Blockflöte
fiddle – Geige
trombone – Posaune
trumpet – Trompete
guitar – Gitarre
saxophone – Saxophon

6 Word groups

places in town
department store, hospital, hostel, leisure centre, police station, restaurant
jobs
engineer, fireman, paramedic, photographer, policewoman, waiter
clothes
dress, jacket, pyjamas, skirt, trainers, trousers
animals
deer, frog, hedgehog, mole, squirrel, woodpecker

Unit 1

1 Definitions

1 four – **wheels**
2 important – country – **capital**
3 places – photos – **sights**
4 woman – king – **queen**
5 spend – hotel – **hostel**
6 live – stage – **concert**
7 piano – use – **instrument**
8 computer – listen – **sound file**

2 Crossword

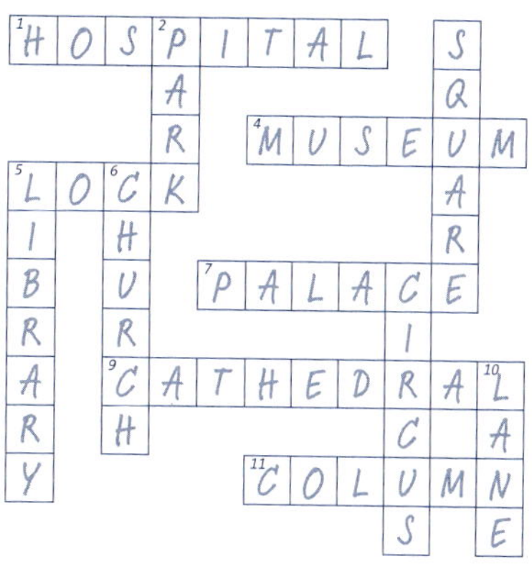

3 Word ladder
more, **move**, **love**, **live**, **like**, **lake**, **late**, **lane**, **line**, **fine**, **mine**, **mile**, milk

4 More about ... London Underground
2 because, *3* only, *4* before, *5* and, *6* but, *7* too, *8* when, *9* more, *10* Although

5 Word friends
do
a good job, a project, nothing
dream
about the teacher, every night, of the future
get
angry, dressed, ready
have
a baby, a cold, enough time
look
after the baby, different, for the money

6 One or two letters?
fi**dd**le, mi**dd**le, stu**d**ent, hi**dd**en, rea**d**y, mo**d**el, a**f**raid, gira**ff**e, tra**ff**ic, o**f**ten, di**ff**icult, le**f**t, a**n**orak, begi**nn**ing, di**nn**er, tu**nn**el, le**n**til, pe**n**cil

7 The fourth word
1 building, *2* vegetable, *3* wet, *4* cellphone, *5* thirsty, *6* queen

8 Word building
1 **dancing lessons** – Tanzstunden
2 **family tree** – Stammbaum
3 **sports gear** – Sportausrüstung
4 **sound file** – Tondatei
5 **ice hockey** – Eishockey
6 **film star** – Filmstar
7 **doorbell** – Türklingel
8 **classroom** – Klassenraum
9 **homework** – Hausaufgabe
10 **wheelchair** – Rollstuhl
11 **firewoman** – Feuerwehrfrau
12 **weekend** – Wochenende

9 Odd word out
1 museum, *2* wheel, *3* CD-player, *4* national, *5* menu, *6* meal

10 The best word
1 angry, *2* shy, *3* proud, *4* puzzled, *5* scared, *6* nervous

11 Word search

S	T	R	A	S	S	E	N	B	A	H	N
U	D	B	A	H	N	H	O	F	M	U	M
E	I	N	S	T	E	I	G	E	N	M	Q
F	L	U	G	H	A	F	E	N	C	S	A
L	F	A	H	R	R	A	D	H	I	T	U
U	Q	F	L	U	G	Z	E	U	G	E	T
G	Q	T	A	X	I	J	Q	H	F	I	O
S	F	A	H	R	P	L	A	N	A	G	P
T	Z	A	U	S	S	T	E	I	G	E	N
E	Z	T	B	U	S	W	U	E	U	N	E
I	U	F	M	S	F	A	E	H	R	E	K
G	G	B	A	H	N	S	T	E	I	G	T

Straßenbahn – tram
Bahnhof – station
einsteigen – get on
Flughafen – airport
Fahrrad – bike
Flugzeug – plane
Taxi – taxi
Fahrplan – timetable
aussteigen – get off
Bus – bus
Fähre – ferry
Bahnsteig – platform
Flugsteig – gate
Zug – train
umsteigen – change
Auto – car

12 Hidden words
1 meal, *2* air, *3* plane, *4* parent, *5* ear, *6* tram, *7* arm, *8* planet, *9* mail, *10* late, *11* learn

13 Word families
1 dream, *2* explain, *3* install, *4* win, *5* laugh, *6* build, *7* describe, *8* rehearse

14 Pronunciation
e – already, bread, breakfast, dead, head, meant
iː – clean, beach, cheap, eastbound, leave, tea
ɪə – dear, appear, clear, ear, hear, idea

15 Opposites
1 national, *2* spicy, *3* clean, *4* right, *5* ending, *6* young, *7* worst, *8* wrong, *9* impossible, *10* leave, *11* rich, *12* closed, *13* quiet, *14* dry, *15* husband, *16* weak

Unit 2 New words ▸ p. 32–35

Mein Handy piepst – es ist eine **SMS**.	My mobile's bleeping – it's a ______________ .
Du kannst mich anrufen, oder **eine SMS schicken**.	You can phone me or __________ me.
Wie du weißt, kann es in Schottland kühl sein.	_______ you know, it can be cool in Scotland.
einen **Dokumentarfilm** über Wales ansehen	watch a ________________ about Wales
Ich **konnte** mit sechs schwimmen.	I was ____________ to swim when I was six.
sich für Pizza oder für Spaghetti **entscheiden**	________________ between pizza or spaghetti

Unit 2 Word pairs ▸ pp. 39–47

Welche Wörter passen zusammen?
*(Alle *Wörter aus Unit 2 sind gekennzeichnet.)*

Unit 3 New words ▸ pp. 56–69

Unsere Schule hat ein neues Hockey**feld**.	Our school has got a new hockey __________ .
Wer **präsentierte** gestern die Sport**nachrichten**?	Who ____________ the sports _______ yesterday?
Heute spielt Liverpool **gegen** den Meister.	Today Liverpool plays _________ the champions.
Dieser **Wald** hat sehr große Bäume.	These ____________ have got very tall trees.
Amerika wurde von Columbus **entdeckt**.	America was ______________ by Columbus.
Darf man in Museen Fotos machen?	Are you ____________ to take photos in museums?
Darf ich bitte das Fenster öffnen?	_______ I open the window please?

Units 4 and 5 New words ▸ pp. 7–11

Er kann nicht singen und **auch nicht** spielen.	He can't sing, and he ca_____ act __________ .
Es ist schade, dass ihr nicht kommen könnt.	__________ that you can't come.
Mein kleiner Hund folgt mir **überall** hin.	My little dog follows me __________ .
Sind Fußballspieler die **Helden** von heute?	Are footballers today's __________ ?
Oje! Ich habe meinen Zug gerade **verpasst**.	Oh dear. I've just __________ my train.
Was **produziert** diese Fabrik?	What does this factory __________ ?
Ausdrücke für einen Urlaub im Ausland lernen	learn __________ for a holiday abroad
einen **Artikel** für eine Zeitung schreiben	write an __________ for a newspaper
Dieses Sofa ist etwas weich, aber **bequem**.	This sofa is a bit soft, but __________ .
Er war so traurig – er hatte **Tränen** in den Augen.	He was so sad – he had __________ in his eyes .
Mit dieser **Maschine** kannst du Brot machen.	You can make bread with this __________ .
Wo kann ich meinen Namen in die Liste **eintragen**?	Where can I __________ my name on the list?

Units 4 and 5 Odd word out

Finde und unterstreiche das Wort, das nicht passt.

1 piano – clarinet – machine – trumpet
2 hero – engineer – doctor – teacher
3 phrase – sentence – paragraph – editor
4 small – comfortable – medium – large
5 paramedic – photographer – performer – produce
6 also – either – article – too
7 eye – ear– tear – nose
8 here – there – everywhere – tomorrow
9 many – miss – much – most
10 pity – pretty – nice – beautiful

Units 4 and 5 Spot the mistakes

In jedem Satz sind zwei Fehler. Unterstreiche und korrigiere sie.

1 I mist my train, so I won't be able to visit you these weekend. missed __________
2 There was snow everywere, so we arriving late at the station. __________ __________
3 It's a real pitty – I real wanted to see you again. __________ __________
4 I haven't see you for weeks, and I haven't seen your mum ither. __________ __________
5 Please tell her I liked the artikel she sent me about football heros. __________ __________

16 Hour glasses

1		F	E	W	
2	W	E	L	S	H
3	C	L	E	A	N
4	F	A	C	T	S
5		A	T	E	
			R		
6		B	I	N	
7	B	A	C	O	N
8	S	K	I	R	T
9	A	F	T	E	R
10		E	Y	E	

1		F	U	N	
2	M	O	N	E	Y
3	T	O	D	A	Y
4	E	N	E	M	Y
5		A	R	M	
			G		
6		A	R	T	
7	S	P	O	O	N
8	F	L	U	T	E
9	S	U	N	N	Y
10		A	D	D	

Das geheime Wort lautet:
Englisch – underground
Deutsch – U-Bahn

17 Picture puzzle
a purse, a dice, a pencil sharpener, a pencil, a helmet, a sandwich, an apple, a fish

Unit 2

1 Word friends
1 eat, *2* wait, *3* dream, *4* read, *5* speak, *6* listen, *7* know, *8* do, *9* become, *10* keep

2 Words with different meanings
1 **name** – Name/benennen
2 **menu** – Speisekarte/Menü
3 **change** – Wechselgeld/umsteigen
4 **single** – ledig/einfache
5 **opposite** – Gegenteil/gegenüber
6 **work** – arbeiten/funktionieren
7 **neat** – gepflegter/tolle
8 **walk** – zu Fuß gehen/Spaziergang

3 Number crossword

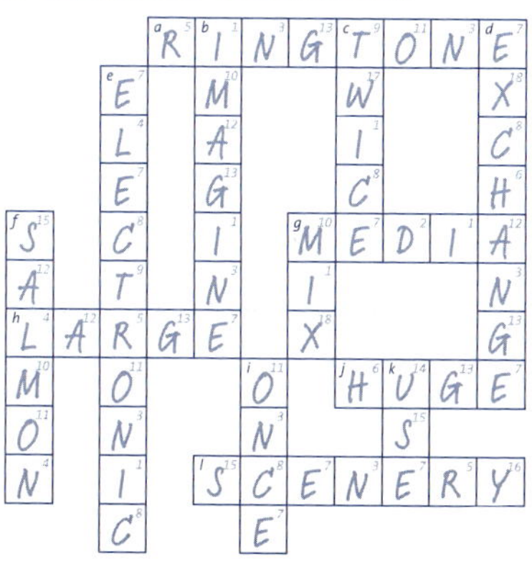

elektronisch – **e** down
riesig – **j** across
zweimal – **d** down
einmal – **i** down
Medien – **g** across
austauschen – **d** down
sich (etwas) vorstellen – **b** down
Landschaft – **l** across

4 Scrambled words: School
1 **timetable** – Stundenplan
2 **teacher** – Lehrer
3 **classmate** – Klassenkamerad/in
4 **holidays** – (Schul-)Ferien
5 **board** – Tafel
6 **science** – Naturwissenschaft

Das geheime Wort lautet: lesson

5 Spot the mistakes
1 <u>biger</u>: bigger, <u>ilands</u>: islands
2 <u>Live</u>: Life, <u>iceland</u>: island
3 <u>have</u>: has, <u>mobil</u>: mobile
4 <u>write</u>: writes, <u>weak</u>: week
5 <u>musik</u>: music, <u>webseite</u>: website

6 Word groups
pets
dog, budgie, cat, fish, guinea pig, hamster, rabbit
media
mobile, television, radio, sound file, magazine, newspaper, video
public transport
timetable, Tube, bus stop, Travelcard, station, ticket machine, tram

7 Making phrases
1 take, *2* send, *3* check, *4* feed, *5* get off, *6* phone, *7* wait, *8* download

8 Opposites
1 empty, *2* ending, *3* forget, *4* important, *5* unfriendly, *6* dry, *7* front, *8* mild, *9* southbound, *10* expensive, *11* last, *12* queen

9 What are the words
1 allowed, *2* able, *3* able, *4* allowed, *5* able, *6* allowed

10 Word pairs

do – course
eat – meal
listen for – phone
pack – rucksack
play – role
play – trombone
read – menu
send – message
turn off – light
walk around – town
wear – helmet

11 Lost words

1 unsafe, *2* healthy, *3* untidy,
4 unhealthy, *5* happy, *6* correct,
7 sorry, *8* sure, *9* unhappy,
10 unsure

12 The fourth word

1 twice, *2* stupid, *3* beauty,
4 flight, *5* forgotten, *6* beginning,
7 translation, *8* wives, *9* knives

13 Odd word out

1 bay, *2* essay, *3* danger,
4 sausage, *5* harbour, *6* sleep,
7 twice, *8* left, *9* join

14 More about ... Orkney

1 islands, *2* on, *3* biggest,
4 and, *5* but, *6* under,
7 another, *8* between, *9* takes,
10 for, *11* make, *12* history

15 The best word

1 exciting, *2* strange, *3* upset,
4 huge, *5* uncool, *6* realistic,
7 surprised

16 Last letter – first letter

1 timetable, *2* excited, *3* detective,
4 elephant, *5* take, *6* elevator,
7 rock, *8* key, *9* you,
10 until, *11* lovely, *12* yawn

17 Word search

A	G	H	I	L	L	R	O	A	D
I	I	F	F	Y	B	A	Y	M	M
U	S	A	B	E	A	C	H	O	J
C	L	R	H	A	R	B	O	U	R
A	A	M	S	E	A	F	C	N	S
S	N	C	L	W	P	I	A	T	Q
T	D	O	A	B	D	E	N	A	U
L	H	A	K	J	U	L	A	I	A
E	B	S	E	B	Q	D	L	N	R
L	Y	T	O	W	E	R	L	X	E

hill – Hügel
road – Straße
bay – Bucht
beach – Strand
harbour – Hafen
sea – Meer
tower – Turm
castle – Schloss
island – Insel
farm – Bauernhof
coast – Küste
lake – See
field – Feld/Sportplatz
canal – Kanal
mountain – Berg
square – Platz

18 Vocabulary network

SCHOOL
do: a test, a project on Scotland, homework
work: alone, in a small group, with a partner
listen to: the CD, an explanation, a recording
SPORTS
play: football, hockey, tennis
go: swimming, riding, surfing
do: judo, sport, yoga
HOBBIES AND FREE TIME
play: the drums, the piano, the trumpet
collect: model cars, postcards, stamps
visit: a friend, grandma, museums

Unit 3

1 What are the words?

1 information – is
2 homework – was
3 is – hair
4 transport – isn't
5 wasn't – furniture
6 is – news
7 is – proof

2 The fourth word

1 twice, *2* harbour, *3* fish,
4 vegetable, *5* captain, *6* season,
7 furniture, *8* shine, *9* instrument,
10 dish

3 Hidden words

1 nose, *2* singer, *3* east,
4 sea, *5* stone, *6* train,
7 star, *8* rain, *9* orange,
10 great, *11* art

4 Word families

a) *2* begin, *3* explain, *4* feel,
5 mean, *6* mix, *7* move,
8 murder, *9* phone, *10* practise,
11 bully, *12* invite, *13* teach,
14 translate
b) *1* meaning, explain
2 invitation, invite
3 practise
4 phone, arrive
5 translation

5 Word friends

exchange
information, euros for pounds,
phone numbers
score
again, three goals, a point
believe
a report, what you read in the newspapers,
everything that people tell you
support
my school team, the players, the coach
train
at a sports club, hard, twice a week

6 Words in pictures

a) *1* face, *2* eye, *3* nose,
4 ear, *5* teeth, *6* hair,
7 mouth, *8* finger, *9* hand
b) *1* pretty/round, *2* blue/bright,
3 long/small, *4* my left/right,
5 broken/white, *6* grey/tidy,
7 a big/loud, *8* clean/strong

7 Definitions

1 washes – hair: **hairdresser**
2 kind – eat: **hostel**
3 team – matches: **supporter**
4 last – winner: **final**
5 sofas – sit: **furniture**
6 most – school: **head teacher**
7 country – pigs: **farmer**
8 place – ship: **quay**

8 Verb forms

1 do – did – done
2 grow – grew – grown
3 take – took – taken
4 win – won – won
5 lose – lost – lost
6 beat – beat – beaten
7 choose – chose – chosen
8 begin – began – begun
9 ride – rode – ridden
10 cut – cut – cut
11 forget – forgot – forgotten
12 let – let – let
13 upset – upset – upset
14 catch – caught – caught

9 Last letter – first letter

1 stress, *2* support, *3* train,
4 news, *5* shirt, *6* travel,
7 leotard, *8* draw, *9* words,
10 shot, *11* tights, *12* station,
13 nothing, *14* goalkeeper,
15 realistic

10 Pronunciation

ə – colour, famous, harbour, nervous
aʊ – around, blouse, house, proud
uː – group, soup, through, you
ʌ – cousin, double, enough, touch
ɔː – bought, course, yours, thought

11 Word ladder

need – **feed** – **feet** – **meet** – **meat** –
beat – **boat** – **boot** – **book** – **took** –
cook – **look** – **lock** – luck

12 More about ... Manchester United

1 club, *2* times, *3* third, *4* over, *5* millions, *6* rich, *7* players, *8* huge, *9* match, *10* even, *11* than, *12* learn

13 Hour glasses

1		S	P	Y	
2	S	P	O	O	N
3	R	U	L	E	R
4	S	H	I	R	T
5		I	C	E	
			E		
6		T	W	O	
7	S	C	O	R	E
8	R	O	M	A	N
9	T	R	A	I	N
10		E	N	D	

1		W	H	O	
2	C	O	A	C	H
3	P	R	I	Z	E
4	H	U	R	R	Y
5		A	D	D	
			R		
6		P	E	N	
7	U	P	S	E	T
8	E	S	S	A	Y
9	S	T	E	E	L
10		A	R	T	

Das geheime Wort lautet:
Englisch – hairdresser,
Deutsch – Friseur/in

14 Scrambled words: sport

1 football – Fußball
2 medal – Medaille
3 champion – Meister
4 helmet – Helm
5 penalty – Strafstoß/Elfmeter
6 goalkeeper – Torwart
7 defence – Verteidigung

Das geheime Wort lautet:
Englisch – leotard,
Deutsch – Gymnastikanzug

15 Word search

G	H	D	S	A	U	S	A	G	E	L	O	C	B	K	R	H	B
O	A	A	P	E	V	O	L	L	E	Y	B	A	L	L	R	E	E
A	M	K	C	S	C	O	U	R	T	J	S	S	O	E	X	L	D
L	B	S	H	A	P	L	A	N	E	F	T	T	U	S	T	I	A
B	U	K	A	L	S	T	A	D	I	U	M	E	S	H	R	C	D
O	R	I	M	A	J	W	G	S	O	C	K	W	E	E	A	O	T
T	G	R	P	D	Z	B	L	S	G	S	K	I	S	L	M	P	I
R	E	T	I	U	W	Y	B	U	S	J	A	X	F	F	Y	T	G
O	R	S	O	F	U	N	D	E	R	G	R	O	U	N	D	E	H
U	F	O	N	T	M	C	Z	C	S	M	S	G	R	A	U	R	T
S	S	U	S	T	E	M	X	H	O	W	Q	P	N	T	W	P	S
E	H	P	H	A	D	S	R	I	F	K	X	C	I	H	A	G	V
R	O	Q	I	D	A	H	W	P	A	F	T	H	T	L	R	Z	F
S	R	X	P	J	L	O	M	S	S	G	A	A	U	E	D	T	E
J	T	S	D	S	X	E	M	C	H	N	B	I	R	T	R	A	R
Y	S	P	A	G	H	E	T	T	I	B	L	R	E	I	O	X	R
Q	P	I	Z	Z	A	K	U	I	P	U	E	G	O	C	B	I	Y
C	U	P	B	O	A	R	D	A	N	O	R	A	K	S	E	N	E

room
bed, chair, cupboard, furniture, shelf, sofa, table, wardrobe

clothes
anorak, blouse, shoe, shorts, skirt, sock, tights, trousers

transport
bus, ferry, helicopter, plane, ship, taxi, tram, underground

sport
athletics, championship, court, goal, medal, skis, stadium, volleyball

food
chips, hamburger, pizza, salad, sausage, soup, spaghetti, stew

16 Odd word out

1 half-pipe, *2* referee, *3* stew, *4* competition, *5* medal, *6* defence, *7* celebrity, *8* industry

17 Crossword

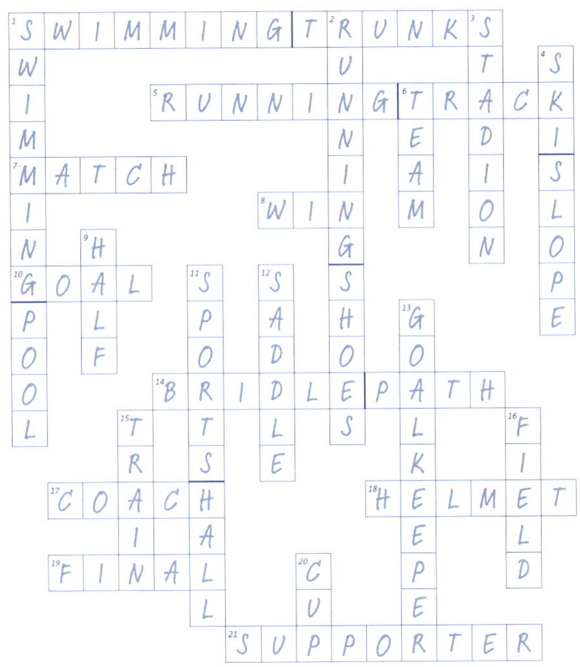

Unit 4

1 Word groups

jobs
actor, cleaner, farmer,
hairdresser, painter,
shop assistant
music
choir, instrument, concert,
musician, song, tune
station
arrivals, passengers, platforms, railway
ticket machines, toilets, trains
weather
cloudy, fog, rain, snow,
stormy, sunny, 20 degrees

2 School words

1 board, *2* choir, *3* class,
4 students, *5* history, *6* biology,
7 pencil, *8* teacher, *9* art, *10* essay

Das geheime Wort lautet:
Englisch – dictionary
Deutsch – Wörterbuch

3 Lost words

1 at, *2* below, *3* on,
4 until, *5* above, *6* to,
7 about, *8* onto, *9* across,
10 about, *11* for, *12* in

4 Word families

1 crowd, *2* danger, *3* difference,
4 electricity, *5* noise, *6* spice,
7 activity, *8* beauty, *9* cloud, *10* industry

5 Last letter – first letter

1 grow, *2* waste, *3* entry,
4 yogurt, *5* traditional, *6* latest,
7 talent, *8* trap, *9* population,
10 nation, *11* neat, *12* translate,
13 exchange, *14* each, *15* helmet

6 Vocabulary network

TRAVEL
visit: a castle, an old church, a museum
pack: a suitcase, a bag, a rucksack
go: by train, on holiday, on a boat trip
SPORT AND FREE TIME
win: a cup, a medal, a prize
go: canoeing, fishing, snowshoeing
wear: running shoes, a helmet, pads
NOT WELL
feel: terrible, ill, weak
have: a sore throat, a cold, a temperature
phone: an ambulance, a doctor, the hospital

7 Word pairs

build – stadium
call – ambulance
climb – mountain
cook – stew
correct – mistake
imitate – somebody's voice
listen to – live music
read – magazine
reply to – questions
score – goal
turn on – light
wear – leotard
win – medal

8 Words with different meanings

1 **square** – Platz/Quadrat
2 **half** – Halbzeit/Hälfte
3 **train** – Zug/trainieren
4 **date** – Datum/ausgehen
5 **hall** – Saal/Flur
6 **final** – Endspiel/letzte
7 **cup** – Pokal/Tasse

9 Word search

R	A	B	B	I	T	H	Y	C	H	U	I	B	G	B
L	N	R	O	N	P	E	W	H	O	C	C	T	I	U
T	W	F	G	P	N	D	H	I	R	D	R	B	R	D
I	U	R	S	A	M	G	A	C	S	Y	O	I	A	G
G	S	W	A	R	O	E	M	K	E	X	C	R	F	I
E	N	F	L	R	L	H	S	E	L	C	O	D	F	E
R	A	R	M	O	E	O	T	N	E	A	D	Y	E	S
K	K	O	O	T	P	G	E	U	P	T	I	X	F	Q
Q	E	G	N	P	C	I	R	S	H	Q	L	C	O	U
R	K	A	N	G	A	R	O	O	A	I	E	O	X	I
H	B	W	N	Z	F	L	I	O	N	Q	S	W	Y	R
I	E	S	W	D	O	G	U	S	T	A	H	J	U	R
N	A	K	W	O	O	D	P	E	C	K	E	R	S	E
O	R	F	S	M	O	U	S	E	R	A	E	L	U	L
M	O	N	K	E	Y	G	O	W	H	I	P	P	O	W

10 Pronunciation

k: **k**nee, **k**nife
h: r**h**ino, r**h**ythm
n: autum**n**, colum**n**
w: ans**w**er, **w**hole
l: fo**l**k music, sa**l**mon
c: s**c**ene, s**c**ience

11 One or two letters?

agree, begin, language, biggest, fog, foggy

cellphone, adult, until, talent, model, pullover

community, swimmer, woman, grammar, moment, thermometer, population, shopping, pepper, supporter, represent, disappear

tomorrow, married, guitar, tired, hurry, directions

basket, essay, glasses, guess, husband, island

bottle, water, pretty, weather, spaghetti

12 More about ... traditional Inuit hunting

1 temperatures, *2* much, *3* fishing, *4* land, *5* just, *6* kind, *7* used, *8* could, *9* built, *10* plus

13 Odd word out

1 minute, *2* lyrics, *3* per cent, *4* text message, *5* build, *6* ready, *7* weigh, *8* local, *9* engineers, *10* café, *11* map, *12* dragon

14 The fourth word

1 kilometre, *2* photographer, *3* theirs, *4* number, *5* instrument, *6* year, *7* moon, *8* knives, *9* shake, *10* sad

15 Spot the mistakes

1 childs: children, has: have
2 realy: really, off: of
3 allso: also, danger: dangerous
4 usualy: usually, errly: early
5 ran: run, swimers: swimmers
6 interresting: interesting, salmons: salmon
7 stand: stands, quitely: quietly
8 bare: bear, jump: jumps

16 Opposites

1 unfriendly, *2* disagree, *3* modern, *4* up, *5* minus, *6* weak, *7* bottom, *8* remember, *9* happy, *10* wife, *11* boring, *12* cold, *13* dirty, *14* upstairs

17 Number crossword

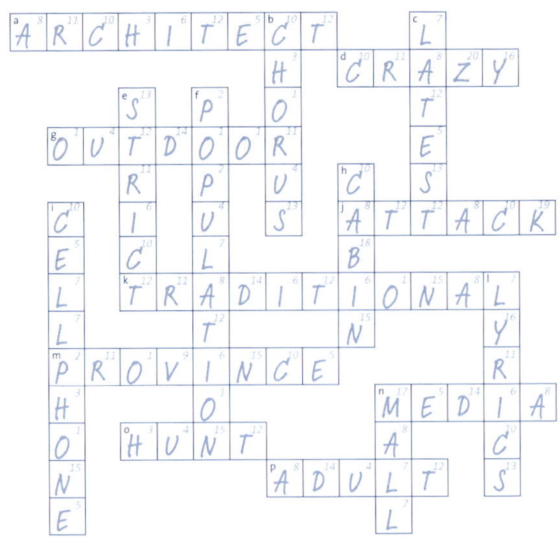

Provinz – **m** across, Hütte – **h** down, Jagd – **o** across, Angriff – **j** across, Erwachsene(r) – **p** across, verrückt – **d** across, streng – **e** down, Einwohnerzahl – **f** down, Einkaufszentrum – **n** down

Unit 5

1 Pronunciation
ʊ – bully, full, pull, put, push, sugar
juː – computer, community, excuse, huge, menu, tube
ʌ – bus, fun, publish, summer, tunnel, trumpet

2 The fourth word
1 vegetable, *2* dish, *3* bird, *4* furniture, *5* clothes, *6* instrument, *7* planet, *8* colour, *9* art, *10* farm

3 Making phrases
1 fall, *2* turn, *3* hang, *4* believe, *5* disagree, *6* grow, *7* look, *8* show

4 Opposites
1 worst, *2* bad, *3* top, *4* dark, *5* unhealthy, *6* unsure, *7* late, *8* untidy, *9* behind, *10* question, *11* below, *12* unfair, *13* right, *14* forget

5 Word families
1 announce, *2* compare, *3* explain, *4* draw, *5* end, *6* live, *7* attack, *8* support, *9* laugh, *10* mean

6 The best word
1 final, *2* strict, *3* artificial, *4* silly, *5* tough, *6* scared

7 Last letter – first letter
1 heroes, *2* success, *3* sights, *4* shadow, *5* worried, *6* drop, *7* painting, *8* grandma, *9* announce, *10* editor, *11* riddle, *12* electric, *13* crazy, *14* yes, *15* section

8 Word search - The media
newspaper – Zeitung
ringtone – Klingelton
record – aufnehmen
magazine – Zeitschrift
editor – Redakteur
programme – Programm
article – Artikel
news – Nachrichten
publish – veröffentlichen
monitor – Bildschirm/Monitor
station – Sender
cellphone – Handy/Mobiltelefon
report – Bericht
headphones – Kopfhörer
television – Fernsehen

9 Words in pictures: fruit and vegetables
1 bright, red, tomatoes
2 large, round, nuts
3 sweet, Spanish, oranges
4 hard, green, apples
5 big, garden, onions
6 delicious, German, strawberries
7 bright, orange, carrots
8 healthy, green, lettuce
9 delicious, new, potatoes
10 long, yellow, bananas

10 Word building
1 pop station: Popsender
2 dance floor: Tanzfläche
3 chat room: Chatroom
4 running shoes: Laufschuhe, Sportschuhe
5 text message: SMS
6 half-time: Halbzeit
7 great-grandfather: Urgroßvater
8 classroom: Klassenzimmer, Klassenraum
9 headline: Schlagzeile
10 wheelchair: Rollstuhl

11 Verb forms
2 blow – blew – blown
3 cost – cost – cost
4 draw – drew – drawn
5 fight – fought – fought
6 grow – grew – grown
7 hang out – hung out – hung out
8 hide – hid – hidden
9 keep – kept – kept
10 shake – shook – shaken
11 sleep – slept – slept
12 wake – woke – woken

12 Hidden words
1 cinema, *2* listen, *3* tram, *4* castle *5* scan, *6* tunnel, *7* uncle, *8* mice, *9* sister, *10* summer/autumn, *11* clean

13 Definitions
1 ears – radio: headphones
2 stop – more: strike
3 spend – home: sleepover
4 corrects – texts: editor
5 person – make: inventor
6 picture – pen: drawing
7 goes – result: success
8 use – voice: microphone

14 What are the words?

1 actor – Schauspieler/in
2 collector – Sammler/in
3 supporter – Anhänger/in
4 farmer – Bauer/Bäuerin
5 visitor – Besucher/in
6 footballer – Fußballspieler/in
7 editor – Redakteur/in
8 reporter – Reporter/in
9 explorer – Entdecker/in
10 inventor – Erfinder/in

15 Word friends

1 squeeze, 2 produce, 3 make, 4 record, 5 play, 6 go, 7 be, 8 have, 9 laugh, 10 skim

16 Scrambled words: American and British English

1 mom, mum
2 cellphone, mobile
3 elevator, lift
4 subway, underground
5 vacation, holidays

17 Hour glasses

1		A	D	D	
2	Q	U	E	E	N
3	U	P	S	E	T
4	F	A	C	T	S
5		T	R	Y	
			I		
6		S	P	Y	
7	U	N	T	I	L
8	Q	U	I	E	T
9	P	R	O	O	F
10		E	N	D	

1		A	T	E	
2	D	I	R	T	Y
3	B	E	A	C	H
4	M	E	D	A	L
5		K	I	D	
			T		
6		B	I	N	
7	C	H	O	I	R
8	F	I	N	A	L
9	S	T	A	G	E
10		I	L	L	

Das geheime Wort lautet:
Englisch – traditional,
Deutsch – traditionell

18 Word ladder

size – **side** – **tide** – **hide** – **ride** – **rude** – **rule** – **role** – **hole** – **mole** – **mile** – **mine** – **line** – **fine** – **file** – film

19 Crossword

Anhang: *Wörter

Unit 1 Lost words
1 time, *2* cheap, *3* whole,
4 guys, *5* royal

Unit 1 Scrambled words
1 coast, *2* flowers, *3* voice,
4 directions, *5* danger

Unit 2 Word pairs
hear – bells, **cut** – hair, **go on** – stage,
watch – documentary, **climb** – rocks,
text – friend, **take part** – event

Units 4 and 5 Odd word out
1 machine, *2* hero, *3* editor,
4 comfortable, *5* produce,
6 article, *7* tear, *8* tomorrow,
9 miss, *10* pity

Units 4 and 5 Spot the mistakes
1 mist: missed, these: this
2 everywere: everywhere, arriving: arrived
3 pitty: pity, real wanted, really wanted
4 see: seen, ither: either
5 artikel: article, heros: heroes